the Original Million Dollar

MERMAID

the Annette Kellerman story

Emily Gibson
with Barbara Firth

ALLEN&UNWIN

To Jamie Thomson
and my mother Margaret Gibson

First published in 2005

Allen & Unwin
83 Alexander Street
Crows Nest NSW 2065
Australia
Phone: (61 2) 8425 0100
Fax: (61 2) 9906 2218
Email: info@allenandunwin.com
Web: www.allenandunwin.com

National Library of Australia
Cataloguing-in-Publication entry:

Gibson, Emily.
   The original million dollar mermaid : the Annette Kellerman
   story.

   Bibliography.
   ISBN 1 74114 432 9.

   1. Kellerman, Annette, 1886–1975. 2. Women swimmers -
   Australia - Biography. 3. Entertainers - Australia -
   Biography. 4. Vaudeville - United States. I. Firth,
   Barbara. II. Title.

797.20092

Set in 11.5/17 pt Requim by Bookhouse, Sydney
Printed by Griffin Press, South Australia

10 9 8 7 6 5 4 3 2 1

CONTENTS

AUTHOR'S NOTE

Much of the information for this book came from newspaper clippings and very old materials, many of which have been archived without the name of the paper, the journalist's name or sometimes the date. So while I've made every endeavour to name all my sources, this has not always been possible. And, reflecting the times through which Annette lived, most measurements quoted in the book are imperial rather than metric.

FOREWORD

In 1952, the first Technicolor water spectacular film *The Million Dollar Mermaid* thrilled the movie-going world. It starred Esther Williams as Annette Kellerman in a Hollywood version of Annette's life. The real Annette Kellerman, aged 66 at the time the film was made, was the film's technical adviser. Guided by Annette, Busby Berkley's choreography was beautiful, amazing and unforgettable. She'd done it all before, in the biggest theatres in the world.

When I saw the film it captivated me, reviving a nascent childhood memory. This was the woman I'd read about in my primary school Australian history book—the first woman to attempt to swim 22 miles across the English Channel in 1905. Having just learnt to dog-paddle myself, I was astonished and she remained somewhere in the recesses of my mind until I saw *The Million Dollar Mermaid*.

I was not a part of Annette's life until just two months before she died. From September 1975, she became very much a part of my life. I became an addendum to hers.

Our first meeting came about through a number of unique, unexpected events and happenings. Looking back it seems like a mystical chain, growing link by link, and leading me to Annette and her sister, Marcelle. Fanciful though this may be, those links produced positive, practical and quite wonderful outcomes for the three of us.

In 1964 I was invited to join the Ladies' Committee of the Sydney Opera House Appeal Fund, which was at that time the most prestigious committee in Sydney. It had been formed as a public relations committee to help raise funds for the building of the Opera House and was an adjunct to the main Appeal Fund Committee. Subsequently, I was appointed honorary public relations officer for the Ladies' Committee.

The Queen opened the Opera House in 1973. Early in 1974, we decided to create the first archives of theatrical memorabilia in Australia. It was a major initiative to collect and preserve our cultural heritage of the performing arts. Two honorary coordinators of the archives were appointed, Mrs Elsa Jacoby MBE and myself.

My public relations activities continued—it was essential to let people know they could now bring family mementos, programs, photos, costumes and bric-a-brac for safe keeping at the Opera House archives. Frank Barnes, general manager of the 'House', called me to his office one day. Publicity was essential, and he wanted to discuss this. He commented that we were going to need something really stunning to give the press to help capture public interest in these archives and asked me for ideas. I suggested we model two of Nellie Melba's gowns on the steps of the House; I had been given these by Hilda Mulligan, MBE, my former teacher of opera stagecraft at the Sydney Conservatorium of Music. On 24 October 1974, the Sydney Opera

House Archives of Theatrical Memoribilia were launched to the public, with the *Sydney Morning Herald* featuring an article and photo of the gowns.

By early 1975 an amazing collection of memorabilia had found its way into the archives. ABC TV asked the committee if we would display some of the collection in a segment on their national program, *This Day Tonight*. We agreed to model gowns and recruited men to wear suitable articles of general interest. It was great fun, shot on the set of *The Importance of Being Ernest* in the Drama Theatre.

In Anglers Paradise on Queensland's Gold Coast, Annette Kellerman and her sister Marcelle saw this program. An excited Annette turned to Marcelle, saying that this was where she wanted her things to go, having first learnt to swim in Cavills Floating Baths in Farm Cove near the Opera House. Both sisters had been widowed and were living together. Apart from friends, few people were aware that Annette and her husband Jimmie had earlier returned from the United States to retire on the Gold Coast. Since Jimmie's death, three years earlier, Marcelle had taken over his role as Annette's scribe and and carer. So Marcelle phoned me at the Opera House and explained that they had seen the television segment and Annette wanted to donate her memorabilia. To me, this was an amazing 'find', and I suggested Marcelle write to the president of our committee, Mrs Marcel (Nola) Dekyvere, CBE, which she did.

At the committee's next monthly meeting in the Opera House boardroom Nola read out Marcelle's letter, which included an invitation for someone to go and select whatever items seemed appropriate. Nola indicated that she thought it would be a waste of time. This surprised me—from the little I knew about Annette at that time I felt there must be something of value in her memorabilia. So I suggested we consult the general manager and be guided by his advice.

I took the letter to Frank Barnes, and he agreed that this was an opportunity not to be missed. He asked if I could go, which I agreed to do with my husband, Gordon.

We spent five extraordinary days on the Gold Coast with these amazing sisters and their helpful friends. The collection was huge and they gave us everything. A furniture van was needed to transport seven big, old cabin trunks full of theatrical and aquatic memorabilia to the Opera House. Our car was also laden with items Marcelle and Annette wanted us to show as soon as we got back.

Annette had turned 89 on 6 July 1975 and we had visited her in September. She was very frail, but after dozing occasionally her indomitable will would resurface and she would carry on telling us about the memorabilia, allowing Gordon to record our conversations about her life, the people she'd known and liked (or not liked!). Much could be written about those five days of discovery. The camerarderie was wonderful, all of us giving our best in the effort to preserve, through Annette's memorabilia, the incredible life of a great Australian woman, athlete and superstar of aquatics, theatre, film and health, who had been a trailblazer and example for women throughout the world.

'Annette Kellerman plays the Sydney Opera House' and 'The mermaid gives up her tail' were some of the headlines that went around the world. News coverage of her donation to the Opera House was amazing. Feature articles appeared in newspapers and magazines. Annette and Marcelle were overjoyed that her mementos had at last found a home. Annette was remembered again as the woman who once, with Melba, was one of the most famous Australian women in the world.

Some years ago, most of the Kellerman collection was transferred from the Opera House to the Powerhouse Museum, and all the paper material is now in the State Library of New South Wales. Prior to the transfer, the Opera House retained me to catalogue the collection under the guidance of its librarian, Paul Bentley.

In 1977, after Annette's death, I researched and coordinated an Opera House exhibition on great swimmers of Australia called 'Splish Splash'. Annette's collection was the genesis for this. Marcelle, then 88, came from Queensland to the opening and was delighted to see Annette featured among all those great champions. As we were leaving, Marcelle stopped on our way to the car. 'Just a minute, Barbara,' she said. 'It's over to you now. I've done all I can for my sister. You know more about Annette than anyone else living. Please tell her story.' I promised her I would.

My commitment to Marcelle has kept me involved ever since, researching Annette in England, Denmark and the United States. Gordon and I researched Annette in public libraries and university libraries on the US east coast in New York, Washington DC and Boston. In Florida at the International Swimming Hall of Fame, we were pleased to see some of Annette's memorabilia from the Opera House collection, which I had sent to them on permanent loan, displayed in Annette's niche there. On the west coast, Los Angeles was our research area and from there I spoke to Esther Williams on the phone. Because we were in different parts of the country and not able to meet, Esther suggested Gordon go to a Radio Shack and obtain a phone bug, then attach it to both the phone and our tape recorder to record our conversations. It worked perfectly! Returning to Australia via New Zealand, we were able to discover more Kellerman material.

Over the years, many people have applied to the State (Mitchell) Library for access to the restricted Kellerman material. This was finally granted to Emily Gibson, who visited me and with whom I could sense a sincere motivation to know more about Annette, as Emily is a year-round daily swimmer. It was an intuitive decision and led to Emily being the catalyst for the making of the documentary, *The Original Mermaid*. Emily became the scriptwriter and I was research consultant for this wonderfully successful film, which gained a nomination at the 2003 Australian Film Industry Awards and was chosen by the prestigious Film Critics Circle of Australia as dual winner for Best Documentary of 2003.

A featured attraction at the Sydney and Melbourne film festivals, the documentary was seen by Jo Paul, commissioning editor for Allen & Unwin Publishers. Jo contacted Emily and then got in touch with me, Annette's authorised biographer. I invited them both to visit me, and granted Emily permission to further access the archival material to help her write this book.

After Annette had passed away, Marcelle often said to me, 'There she is, sitting up there on her little pink cloud, still directing everbody!' When she had scattered Annette's ashes over the Barrier Reef, as Annette had requested, Marcelle said simply, 'Thanks everyone—mission accomplished.'

For the publication of this biography, I echo Marcelle's words to all the people involved in all the links which enabled Emily and me to tell Annette's story: thanks everyone—mission accomplished.

Barbara Firth

1
THE PERFECT WOMAN

It was a Monday morning in the summer of 1908 and Dr Dudley Sargent, director of the Hemenway Gymnasium at Harvard University, was breakfasting with his wife.

'Here's someone to add to your list of hopefuls,' his wife said, reading out loud from her newspaper, 'Australian woman swimmer arrested at Boston Beach'.

The article went on to describe how a young girl, who was about to begin a distance swim from the beach, had been arrested for exposing her bare legs in public. She was wearing a man's one-piece bathing suit, which in court she subsequently claimed to be *de rigueur* in her own country. Other long-distance feats of the young athlete listed in the article included swimming the River Thames and the Yarra River in Melbourne, Australia. She had also spent more than ten hours battling huge waves in the English Channel.

On hearing this, the doctor put down his coffee cup and stood up.

'I have to find that woman.'

'But dearest, you have twenty women lined up outside in the vestibule,' protested his wife.

'I don't care!' he replied, throwing down his napkin and walking out.

The doctor, a thorough and meticulous man, never acted on hunches. In fact, from 1883 to this very Monday in 1908 he had been conducting a series of painstakingly rigorous scientific tests designed to determine the exact proportions of the Perfect Woman, including testing the lung capacity of almost 10 000 women. His quest was to find, if not a living, breathing Venus de Milo, then the closest human specimen to her. His Harvard colleagues had joked with him that he had chosen a particularly fine area of research to undertake. The doctor pointed out to them that measuring 10 000 women was not all it was cut out to be. So far, none of them had come close to his ideal, and at the sight of his tape measure the young women behaved strangely, becoming crippled with shyness or over-excited and flirtatious— neither of which made it easy for him to do his job properly.

That summer, Annette Kellerman seemed to be everywhere in Boston. Doctor Sargent needed only to have raised his eyes for a moment and his gaze would have met, on any number of posters plastered about town, the words: 'Annette Kellerman, the Australian Mermaid performing live at Wonderland.' 'Wonderland' was a huge amusement park on Revere Beach where Annette gave exhibitions of diving and swimming as often as ten times a day. On his way to Annette Kellerman's concession—the space allotted for her to perform her act—he would have passed some of Wonderland's less salubrious attractions—The House of Infant Incubators, 'a scientific, humanitarian and educational institution', and the House of Follies next door. If she was not in her dressing-room, the doctor would have found Annette out rough riding with Major Gordon W. Little and the Pawnee from his Great Wild West Show. The Major had been a bank president and his wife was a graduate of Smith College, but they preferred to spend their time touring the country with the Native Americans he had lived with for 30 years.

Waiting outside with all the other fans after the show, Dr Sargent finally managed to convince Annette's father, Frederick Kellerman, that he was a genuine professor. Frederick took the doctor inside and introduced him to Annette. The professor wasn't disappointed. When he told her of his research, she laughed and said: 'Why not?'

Annette stood in Dr Sargent's office in her bathing suit as the doctor placed a card on the table and proceeded to extract a tape measure from his trouser pocket. He asked her to stand still while he took her measurements. As he measured every inch of her, from her head to her wrist to her big toe, he told her a little of the scope of his work. He had begun research into finding the perfect proportions of the human body in 1887 and since then had measured almost 10 000 women. The information was stored in a card system of his own devising. He not only measured Annette thoroughly, but asked her for her date and place of birth, father's occupation and both the nationalities and the causes of death of her parents. 'But they're not dead yet!' she exclaimed.

The doctor then tested Annette's lungs, making her breathe into a rubber balloon and marvelling at her capacity. She didn't feel marvellous—just cold and a little like a guinea pig. Finally, the professor handed her a Navaho rug to wrap herself in and led her up on to a platform in a Harvard lecture theatre where she stood before a room full of eager students.

'Dr Sargent took off the rug and I was left standing in my little one-piece bathing suit,' she later wrote in her unpublished autobiography, 'My Story'.

As Annette stood there shivering, the doctor went on to give a complete lesson on 'The Female Form Divine'. 'I want you to carry this figure in your minds,' he was reported as saying to the 200 or more students. 'And in all your work keep it as an ideal of what a woman's figure should be.' He declared her to be:

> a model for all young women to pattern by her beauty of outline and artistic proportions. Miss Kellerman has an appealing comeliness and at the same time has an all round development very superior to any woman I have ever seen. I will say without qualification that Miss Kellerman embodies all the physical attributes that most of us demand in The Perfect Woman.

Though Annette Kellerman joked about the title at the time, later telling reporters 'I'm perfectly healthy, that's all,' she had in some ways been preparing for this moment all her life.

As a child, she had reason to feel far from perfect. Annette Sarah (after her mother's friend Sarah Bernhardt) Kellerman was born on 6 July 1886 at 101 Victoria Street, Darlinghurst in Sydney. She was a fat, happy baby with big blue-grey intelligent eyes and lots of energy. While she tried to walk very early, by the time she was two she still had not managed to stay upright. Her legs were bowed and couldn't hold her. Annette was diagnosed with rickets and until she was seven was made to wear heavy iron braces on her legs.

Annette remembered them hurting and, at every opportunity, she'd try to take them off. Her parents would often
find her huddled in the corner of a room reading a fairytale,
escaping from the pain and discomfort. Lost in this make-
believe world, Annette imagined herself not only as the
physically perfect and beautiful heroine of the story, but also
as the reckless and daring Prince Charming—riding and fencing
his way to rescue the princess. Later, Annette was to play both
hero and heroine, accomplishing her own feats of daring in
both roles.

From an early age she realised she was different from her
older brother Maurice, her younger sister Marcelle and little
Fred. She couldn't run and play like other children. Her mother,
who always blamed herself for her daughter's infirmity because
she'd gone swimming on the day Annette was born, was strict
with the others but far less so with her. Her sister Marcelle later
said, 'My mother could never say no to Annette.'

Annette soon worked out that being different meant a lot
more attention. And there were always plenty of guests at her
family home to satisfy her need to be noticed.

Frederick and Alice Kellerman were both musicians and
socialised with Sydney's élite arts set at the turn of the twentieth
century. Annette, who longed to be an actress, would often be
allowed to stay up late and meet the guests. She learned how
to work the room at an early age, observing her mother in action.

'Mum had that way of getting people to do things,' said
Marcelle, when questioned about her mother's forceful personality.

Alice Charbonnet had been born in Cincinatti in 1860 to
an American mother and a French father. He was Judge Amable
Charbonnet, the roving Chief Justice of French Possessions and
Colonies in the South Pacific. In some ways, Alice's childhood

growing up in the tropics is mirrored in her daughter's most famous films, where the heroine dives and swims and wanders through tropical paradise.

When Alice came to Australia from Paris in 1879 she was already a promising young concert pianist and composer, having studied at the Paris Conservatoire with Cecile Chaminade, one of the first established woman composers in France.

Melbourne was hosting Australia's inaugural International Exhibition and Alice had been sent by the French government to demonstrate Pleyel and Erard pianos. During this time she met Nellie Mitchell, who later became known as Nellie Melba. Alice taught Nellie to accompany herself on the piano and they soon became firm friends. Alice was undoubtedly an impressive musician and, from the photos of her at this time, very much a Parisienne.

The chic salons of Paris must have seemed a long way from the rather gauche society and slightly shabby drawing rooms of Melbourne and Sydney. However, Alice discovered in Sydney that social occasions became *very* chic whenever a certain Frederick Kellerman was present. There was nothing gauche or shabby about Frederick, a young violinist who was already well known in the musical circles of Sydney. Tall and handsome, Frederick favoured a top hat, a Prince Albert coat and pinstriped trousers. His German father had a leather goods shop in the city but had greater ambitions for his son. Frederick was taught violin and became a master of harmony and counterpoint.

When the pianos were put on the boat back to Paris Alice Charbonnet was not with them. Frederick and Alice were both young, talented and ambitious, and when they opened their Conservatoire de Musique at 43 Philip Street, right in the heart of the city, it was an instant success. With August Wiegund, the

Belgian organist who had come to play the famous organ at the new Sydney Town Hall, they founded the Sydney Orchestral Society. They were also involved in the birth of the Australian Musical Association and the Sydney Philharmonic. The Kellerman soirées attracted all the most important musical and artistic figures in Sydney—visiting international actors and writers mingled with local musicians and artists.

'Madame Kellerman's "At Home" on Tuesday afternoon was a crush,' wrote the local *Sunday Times*. 'You couldn't get in at one door, and then having got in you couldn't get out the other. Everybody was there. All the talk, pretty loud too (the music couldn't get a word in edgeways) was of "frocks and Federation". We sat two together on chairs or three together on stairs. We took our tea standing in the hall, or squeezed up against agreeable people in tiny corners. Everything was unconventional and delightful. "Vive la vie Boheme!"'

It was absolutely *the* place to be. A three-storey terrace house with almost every room given over to the teaching of music, the Conservatoire offered lessons in every kind of music. There were six pianos, two on each floor.

During the day, the house in Philip Street was filled with music as the students were taught their various instruments. Every room contained a student practising on a different instrument. The noise echoed through the large, high-ceilinged rooms and vibrated along the wooden floorboards, despite the Persian rugs scattered through the house. Annette, too, was supposed to be practising the piano or the violin. In 'My Story', Annette described the experience as 'torture'.

As she grew older, she would find a room far from where her mother and father were teaching, take out her favourite fairytale book and read it with one hand. With her other, she played her five-finger piano exercise over and over again. A photo of her at the time shows a very serious and rather plain, pale young girl seated next to her much healthier and prettier sister.

After five years the braces finally came off Annette's legs, however she was still too weak to walk properly. At a time when the medical vogue was to operate or apply complicated and often torturous stretching and strengthening devices, Frederick and Alice were lucky to find a doctor who prescribed swimming as a cure. Frederick, unable to swim himself, was not totally convinced of the doctor's prescription until one day, while out sailing, he fell overboard. When his brother Emile pulled him in, Frederick was remarkably calm. He'd enjoyed his time in the water and had marvelled at its buoyancy. He decided to follow the doctor's prescription for his daughter. Annette, like most children, hated her medicine.

'I loathed it,' she said. 'They had to drag me kicking and screaming to the lessons.'

Neither parent realised how much this event would change not just their daughter's fate but that of the whole family.

From the side of the pool where she held on for dear life, Annette watched her brothers and sister take to the water with ease. After five or six lessons they were swimming like seals. It took Annette eighteen lessons and was a painfully slow process. By then she was determined not just to learn to swim but to be the best. By the age of seven she had built herself a strong new pair of legs and had begun to beat not only her siblings but everyone else.

Only a cripple can understand the intense joy that I experienced when little by little I found that my legs were growing stronger and taking on the normal shape . . . After I learned, I'd go swimming anywhere, any time, at the drop of a hat.

On hot Sydney summer mornings as she walked to school Annette passed the baths where she had learned to swim. It was a short walk from Philip Street through the Botanical Gardens to Cavill's Floating Baths at Farm Cove, right next to where the Sydney Opera House stands today.

'It took a lot of my willpower to keep on the road to the convent. I found it got weaker and weaker until I was more often at the pool than at class,' Annette said.

Marcelle, or Mipps as she was known in the family, recalled that school studies were seen as just a waste of time by Annette, who wanted to be outside doing something, using up her surplus energy. Annette was easily bored, and trouble usually started when she became restless and said to Mipps: 'Let's do something!' One day, while they were waiting for a nun who was late for class, Annette persuaded all the kids to hide behind a huge stack of chairs at one end of the classroom. 'As usual, we all did as she said—she had that gift,' Mipps recalled. When the teacher finally arrived, she found an empty room and, convinced the children's giggling was the sound of hundreds of squeaking rats, ran from the room.

Annette liked to be the centre of attention, and performing was one way she could attract it. Sometimes Mipps was her only audience. Annette would grab her sister by the arm and drag her to the tram shed, where she would dress up in her mother's clothes and make Mipps watch as she paraded around. Just as abruptly, Annette would leave her sister and run away, 'off on a high adventure—no doubt to some gorgeous festivity, out the back gate or down the back lane,' according to Mipps.

At school, Annette was absent far more often than she was present. When she had almost finished her 'time' at The Ladies' Finishing School, which she attended after St Patrick's, the headmistress, who was driven to her wit's end by the lively Annette, finally worked up the courage to tell Mr Kellerman that it might be a good idea if he removed his daughter from school, in the interests of all concerned.

It seemed no one could stop Annette from doing whatever she wanted—and what she wanted most was to be in the water. With the harbour beaches all around her she could swim every day.

Swimming in Australia, unlike in Europe or America, was commonplace. Robert Hughes' book *The Fatal Shore* reports that visitors from London in the 1850s wrote home about the children of the convicts spending all day at the beach 'swimming like dab-chicks'.

In other countries, swimming was a sport almost totally restricted to men, who—like Byron, who swam the Hellespont, and Captain Matthew Webb, the first man to swim the English Channel—used the breaststroke to accomplish these feats of endurance. Annette swam the double-armed trudgeon, a version of the Australian crawl and a much faster and more efficient way to move through the water.

At the turn of the century Sydney would have been a great place to learn to swim. Cavill's was just one of the many baths that were springing up all along the Sydney coastline. Swimming clubs would either net off sections of the harbour or build permanent rock pools. Almost every beach in Sydney still has at least one or more netted areas or rock pools—Coogee Beach has four.

Cavill's Baths was a section of harbour coastline enclosed by shark-proof netting suspended on floating pontoons. On top of these were dressing-rooms and a walkway with diving platforms of various heights. The baths were located off the sandstone sea wall at Farm Cove. Rolling lawns swept down to the water's edge and splendid old Moreton Bay figs grew close by and shaded the bathers. From the baths, swimmers could glance up and see the old sandstone prison island of Fort Denison and, across the harbour, the magnificent governor's residence at Kirribilli. Percy Cavill, Annette's teacher, was one of the six sons of Frederick Cavill, all of them world-class or world-champion swimmers. Frederick himself had attempted to swim the English Channel, and his sons had followed in their father's wake, teaching the Australian crawl and butterfly at home and abroad. Also training at the pool were Snowy Baker and his brother Frank. Only a couple of years older than Annette, Snowy was already one of the best divers in the country. Like Annette, he starred in some early movies in Australia before heading to Hollywood where he became a stuntman and a coach to the stars. He taught Johnny Weismuller, who played the first Tarzan, to dive, swing through the trees and wrestle crocodiles.

Annette watched Snowy every morning while she was learning to swim and was mesmerised by the beauty of his dives. Once she had mastered swimming and was beating all the boys, it was all she wanted to do.

'Snowy Baker dared me to go off the high platform, so up I went,' wrote Annette. 'I suppose it was about 30 feet high but when I got up the top it looked a hundred. My legs were quivering, but I made up my mind that I would not come down the ladder and be laughed at, so I swallowed hard and took the plunge.'

'She was quick *and* fearless,' Frank Baker was later quoted as saying. 'The first time she tried to copy Snowy diving, she hit the water all wrong. She lay there until she got her breath and then she climbed the ladder again. Then she leapt out. It was perfect. She entered the water like an arrow, and from that time on, I don't think she ever made anything but clean dives.'

Once Annette entered the water she underwent a kind of Protean metamorphosis—she was transformed from crippled child to beautiful mermaid, from weakling to superwoman, from colonial curiosity to international sensation. A photo of her at this time in a tutu, balancing on one pointed ballet shoe, shows a totally different child to the pale, serious little girl with leg braces. She is beautiful, flashing a confident and slightly mischievous smile. Like a character in one of her fairytales she changed from ugly duckling to beautiful princess.

Even if she felt fear, it was not apparent to those watching. She could dive from the highest platforms, swim faster and stay under water longer than anyone else at the baths. Once she overcame rickets, Annette realised she could train her new body to do anything and was determined to keep it that way. Just as an opera singer sees their voice as a precious instrument, Annette felt enormous respect for her body. She would spend her life looking after it, and kept age and illness at bay by keeping her body as pure as a temple—no alcohol, cigarette smoke or red meat were ever allowed inside its sacred portals. She never wanted to be that sickly little girl again. Annette swam and practised ballet and, when she had time, walked 10 miles a day. Interestingly, when writing about her body in her memoirs, she always refers to it in the third person.

'Her extraordinary physique,' she wrote in 'My Story', 'which she had developed through swimming and dancing, made a great impression wherever she went.'

For someone who was remarkably pragmatic and down to earth about most things, Annette always spoke of water and swimming as magical. The almost didactic language of her self-help manuals, *How to Swim* and *Physical Beauty: How to Keep It*, both published in 1918, suddenly switches to the romantic and dreamy when she mentions water. Like the fairytales she read to escape from her pain and music as a child, she saw water and swimming as an escape from 'a black earth full of people that push'.

After her crippled childhood, the experience of having created a body over which she had almost absolute control gave Annette a certain invulnerability. She would have plenty of accidents throughout her career—she always did her own stunts—but she would emerge virtually unscathed. To the mass of women laced into corsets beneath weighty skirts—especially to those who craned their necks to look up at Annette in her scanty swimsuit atop the 90 foot diving board—she must have seemed from another world. Salacious interest in her near-nakedness was outstripped by the sheer sensation of her act. As she flew through the air in her daredevil dives, she appeared to be a creature entirely liberated from the earthbound audience.

Back when she was growing up in Sydney, diving and swimming, Annette was simply having fun. There was no thought of becoming a professional swimmer. In later years, her brothers played violin professionally in Paris and her parents had planned for her to go there too and be tutored by the best teachers, but Annette had other plans—she wanted to be either a famous actress or ballerina.

Annette had taken up ballet at much the same time as swimming, but it was ballet she really loved. She was also sure her mother's companions in Paris would help her to be an actress. In the drawing room where the Kellermans held their soirées was a stage with two grand pianos on it and above them three portraits of her mother's friends that Annette would stand in front of and gaze at endlessly. One was of Cecile Chaminade and another of Nellie Melba, but it was the middle painting she especially admired—a life-size portrait of Sarah Bernhardt on which was addressed in French: 'To the charming Alice Charbonnet with great affection—Sarah Bernhardt'. She would plague her mother with questions about Bernhardt and when she was coming to visit.

Bernhardt never did make it to one of the Kellerman soirées, but George Rignold, a famous London actor, did. Annette, who was ten at the time, begged her mother to let her perform for him. And when she wanted something she didn't let up until she got it. Mipps described the incident in a 1976 television documentary:

> I think it was this tenacity she had. She never gave way on anything at all . . . nobody counted, nothing counted, none of us or anybody counted. What counted was she wanted to get to the top of the tree. George Rignold was a very famous English actor and of course mother being at the head of music and arts and that sort of thing, he came over quite often. So Mum said to him, 'I would like you very much to do something for me if you would.' He said, 'I'll be only too pleased.'

Alice told Rignold that she wanted to put on a little performance with her children 'and there's one especially who wants to show you how special she is'.

'And so we put on a show of *Macbeth* and there was Annette . . . I was only the nurse carrying a candle or something,' recalled Mipps, 'and here was Annette going around saying 'Out, out damned spot.'

Annette may have become a popular amateur theatrical actress, or may even have gone on to the Sydney stage as a professional, but those dreams were scuttled by the economic depression which hit Australia at the turn of the twentieth century. The Kellermans were especially hard hit. Parents were no longer able to afford the luxury of music lessons, and students left the Conservatoire in droves.

By this time Annette was fourteen and easily beating all the girls at the baths; she was even winning races against the best of the men. Percy Cavill, Snowy Baker and brother Frank had been fighting a losing battle for the last couple of years trying to persuade Frederick Kellerman that his daughter should compete in the professional championships.

'We knew we had a winner,' said Frank Baker, 'and we encouraged Annette to swim competitively.' Mr Kellerman would always politely but firmly decline, stating: 'No daughter of mine will support herself in that manner.'

That changed when Kellerman realised that his daughter may be able to help the family out financially. He had more time on his hands now the Conservatoire had closed, and he began to attend some of his daughter's swimming meets. He was there when Annette flew off the platform and plunged into the water for the 100 yards final against an all-male lineup. She won easily and broke the record. At fifteen, she established a new world record for swimming a mile, and he was standing on the sideline with all the other parents. Kellerman was finally persuaded to let his daughter swim professionally. 'Father took up my training in a systematic fashion and through thick and thin saw that I stuck to it,' she wrote in 'My Story'.

The Baker brothers now took the opportunity to convince Kellerman to allow Annette to dive from higher platforms. She was already diving from 40 feet, which was something no girl had ever attempted. He gave his permission reluctantly, but Alice Kellerman didn't like it at all. She was horrified at the thought of her daughter racing and diving half-naked against all those men.

In the meantime Annette was enjoying herself immensely. She liked to win and it was easy for her. Though she was swimming professionally, she was only making enough to shout her friends a milkshake after school. Her mind was still focused very much on a career on the stage. She yearned to gain her mother's approval by being a brilliant actress or a prima ballerina—then she would be good enough to join, as an equal, the other guests at her mother's soirées.

But the Kellerman soirées vanished from the Sydney social scene once the pupils stopped coming to the Conservatoire. The family moved to Melbourne, hoping to find more work there. Alice began teaching at Mentone College for girls, but Frederick had less luck. Reluctant to tell the family how bad the financial situation was, or to complain about the constant pressure in his chest, he struggled into his suit and top hat and set out on his bicycle every day to try to find work teaching, but returned home without securing one pupil. In 1903 he suffered his first serious heart attack.

In many ways, the depression and the heart attack brought the family closer. The children could see how difficult it was for their parents, and tried to think of ways to make money. Annette realised she would have to give up her dreams of the stage, at least for the moment, and concentrate on making a living with her swimming. She began training in the Yarra River with her father standing by with a stopwatch. First she attempted a mile, then a few days later she swam 2½ miles. It was a warm day and the sun was shining through the trees on either bank. Though the day was fine the Yarra, like most Australian rivers, was milky brown. Annette's father and some of her friends accompanied her in a launch and her progress was watched with interest by people out for a walk along the river and some early morning rowers. News spread quickly and soon the papers caught on: 'A notable feat was accomplished on Saturday by Miss Annette Kellerman . . . who swam 2 miles 21 chains in the Yarra River in the record time of 46 minutes 32.5 seconds.'

She kept up such a strong steady pace that her father suggested she 'take it easy', but Annette, in fine form, instead asked those in the accompanying boat whether they were getting tired. She felt so good after this swim—'I prefer long distances; I think it's rather good fun,' she was quoted as saying—that she decided to try 5 miles. And when she completed a 10 mile swim, it was officially recorded as the longest ever swum by a woman.

It was around this time that Annette and Mipps visited a display of tropical fish at the Melbourne Exhibition Hall, which had been built to house the 1880 International Exhibition. It was an impressive building with Gothic transepts and a huge dome rising 223 feet above the floor, with natural clerestory lighting. The aquarium tank below the dome looked a little insignificant in the scale of things, being only 20 feet long, 10 feet wide and 6 feet deep. Mipps joked that her sister should dive into the tank and swim with the fish. According to her, Annette took the proposition literally and climbed up the side and dived in while Mipps went around with a hat. What is more likely is that David Mitchell, the father of Nellie Melba, who had built the Hall, gave Annette the opportunity to swim there.

In any case, she was so popular that she began performing every weekend, drawing large crowds of people. This was the place where her mother had played the grand piano twenty years earlier, dressed in the height of Parisienne couture. Now Alice Kellerman could only demur. 'My mother was upset when my first job was swimming around with the eels and seals in the Melbourne Aquarium,' Annette said later in her memoirs.

Annette very quickly realised that if she had to swim she could turn it into a spectacular performance. Lady Macbeth's mad scene might not work too well underwater, but she could do a show—and she would make it a good show. She had already discovered that ballet made her diving more graceful and skilful, so she combined the two. Having learned to hold her breath for long periods of time, Annette was able to create a mermaid character, to the amazement of the crowds. She had invented something entirely new and throughout her career she was to perfect this and raise it to an art form.

It was at the Princes Court, an amusement park situated on a bridge over Melbourne's Yarra River, that she gave her first display of what would become her trademark on the American vaudeville circuit and later on screen. Sitting high up on a platform in a glittering green and silver mermaid tail, Annette looked down and saw an audience looking back up at her, entranced— and there, in the front row, was her mother. She was so nervous that she hardly heard the gasps and applause as she slid at astonishing speed down a slide into the darkened pool. Annette was determined to stay underwater for as long as she could before emerging triumphant. With no sign of the star performer, the audience soon became restive. After one and a half minutes, some of the men in the crowd were looking anxiously down at the water. One had actually begun to take off his shirt and was preparing to dive in when all at once the missing mermaid resurfaced. She had been down for more than two minutes. The applause was deafening and over the top of it all she could hear a distinctly French voice calling 'Bravo. Bravo, ma petite!'

Annette continued to entertain the now captive audience with displays of balletic dives and diverse swimming styles. For two shows a day she earned the princely sum of £10 a week.

Not long after this, Annette and her father were introduced to Bland Holt, of the Royal Theatre in Melbourne, who was putting on a lavish production of the play *Breaking of the Drought*. A master of stagecraft and effects in the days when there was little technology backstage, Holt was known as far away as London for his remarkable scenic effects and striking design. When he asked Annette to star in a scene which recreated Bondi Beach, Marcelle says she gasped: 'At last, I'll be on the stage.'

The pool in which she was to perform was sunken into the stage, and it was here that she was involved in the first of a long series of close shaves that punctuated her career. After one performance Annette was showing off some dives and got carried away, literally. The tank was emptied after every performance and, not noticing that the pumps had been turned on, she found herself caught in a whirlpool as she was sucked towards the tiny outlet pipe. 'Fortunately I had the presence of mind to catch the end of a beam projecting over the side and, screaming hard, managed to attract attention,' she later wrote. A stagehand heard her and shut down the pumps with just seconds to spare. Mipps, writing 60 years later, still believed it was all her sister's fault because of her 'surplus of self confidence to do stupid but outrageous stunts'.

Annette was being paid a reasonable wage for a seventeen-year-old girl, but it was still not enough to support the family. Furthermore, after *Breaking of the Drought* finished its run, and she had broken all the records in swimming and in diving, there was not much left for Annette to achieve.

'In Australia swimming is so much a sport for everyone,' she wrote, 'that the very abundance of the sport makes it commonplace.'

In an interview with *The New Idea* at around this time, Annette mentioned that she had broken all the records for ladies' swimming in Australia and 'as far as I know for English swimmers too'. She would have been seventeen years old but her confidence is remarkable. Though swimming was commonplace, lifesaving was not, and Annette had strong views on the subject, which she expressed in the interview: 'It doesn't follow that because anyone can swim that they can save life, but I think they ought to learn.' When describing the etiquette of lifesaving, she is very matter of fact. 'Suppose the person to be saved throws a loving arm around your neck, what then?' the interviewer asked her while they sat on the steps at Cavill's Baths.

'Oh you musn't let them,' replied Miss Kellerman, promptly. 'I've hauled lots of them out and no one's ever got an arm around my neck. If they are too flurried to reason, you must hit them quickly in the face or body like this.' And Miss Kellerman flung herself at her companion, turned her over, 'saved' her most vigorously and unceremoniously and towed her to the steps.

Hearing of Annette's exploits in the Yarra, Sydney's 'swimming elite'—the Cavill brothers and Snowy Baker—used their powers of persuasion by mail to make Frederick Kellerman realise that the only place for Annette was England. They believed she was ready to try her luck at swimming the English Channel. Frederick was finally convinced when an acquaintance came back from England with news of a big Channel swim to commemorate a Captain Webb's first crossing 30 years earlier. Frederick saw more possibilities for making money in a country where swimming was still a novelty. Though Annette was simply delighted to be going to England, for her father it was a difficult decision and a huge gamble—he would be leaving the family thousands of miles behind in the hope that his daughter might find success and riches in an unknown land. Alice and he discussed it, and decided that they should leave as soon as possible.

'So mother and father raised £40 for the fare from a benefit concert, and in 1904 I set off with my father to swim back the family fortune,' Annette said.

2
SWIMMING BACK THE FAMILY FORTUNE

Passengers taking a stroll on the third day out to sea from Sydney were becoming accustomed to the sight of a young lady marching around and around the ship's decks at a cracking pace, usually followed by one or more young men. Not all those sunning themselves in their deckchairs approved.

'That's the third time she's passed by this morning. I'm becoming rather tired of that young lady's antics,' one passenger was heard to remark to her paid travelling companion.

'I think she's just taking in the sea air,' her companion responded timidly.

'Taking in the young men more likely, trailing them after her like so many trophies.'

'Oh no,' said the companion. 'She seems such a nice girl. I'm sure she's just full of beans.'

'Full of airs and graces, more like.'

Mr Frederick Kellerman, sitting close by with the pale face of an invalid and a blanket over his knees, was also perturbed by the attention his daughter was calling to herself. Of course *she* was quite innocent, but some of the young men who tagged along behind her on her promenades were decidedly not.

Frederick had been suffering a series of what the doctors described as 'heart attacks' before and since he had left Sydney. Today, they would probably be put down to angina. His doctor had advised against the trip. Alice had agreed but was unable to persuade her husband. As the ship had moved out of the dock, she had waved tragically, sure she would never see Frederick again. However, he was an optimist—a characteristic his daughter had inherited in bundles, he thought, as she marched by with her entourage in tow.

As she was unable to swim during the voyage, walking was how Annette kept herself fit. Her preferred distance was 10 miles, but sometimes she would settle for 5. She was also unbeatable at deck quoits. After a five-course meal at the captain's table and plenty of joking about who was going beat her at quoits, this alarmingly healthy and happy Australian would still have energy to burn, foxtrotting with one and quickstepping with another admirer until they fell back into their chairs, exhausted, marvelling at her stamina. There was one young New Zealander who could keep up with her on the deck and the dance floor. They took to walking, at a rather slower pace, around the decks on moonlit nights and dancing until the musicians stopped and began packing up. She was eighteen, he wasn't much older and the setting was storybook romantic. Writing about this time Annette called it 'puppy love' and a result of 'tropical moonshine' but it was serious enough for Kellerman to whisk his broken-hearted daughter off the ship at Naples.

'Remember you've a lot to do before you settle down,' he told her. 'There's plenty of time for moonshine later on.'

Annette was angry and upset as they travelled overland to London, but later recalled that it only took a few weeks to get over the New Zealander. It was London, not the lost New Zealand love, that she claimed as 'the bitterest disappointment' in her life. Arriving on a dark foggy Sunday, Annette recalled 'the streets were as still as the dead'.

It was a nasty shock after sunny Australia. The Kellermans found accommodation in Gower Street right near the West End, with Bloomsbury, the British Museum and the newly opened Royal Academy of Dramatic Art close by. But amidst the street's grand façades and large houses they were only able to afford a gloomy little hotel. It was not just the weather that was discouraging. They had just settled in when their hopes of fame and glory were quickly dashed. London boasted plenty of swimming clubs, both indoor and outdoor—many more than in Australia. In fact, the first indoor swimming club opened in London in 1742 and since then they had proliferated. What Kellerman and his daughter discovered as they approached the various clubs was that to be a professional athlete in England was an 'unpardonable sin' as Annette later described it. It seemed that there was no chance of Annette performing as a professional in a country where an amateur was seen as superior. Only the rich and privileged were able to maintain an amateur status— if you were a paid athlete, you were definitely lower class. 'Professional swimmers up to that time had been persons who wore gorgeous tights and had a cockney swagger,' one journalist of the time noted. Most poor people didn't swim. The closest they would have come to it was the local bathhouse, where they went once a week (once a fortnight in winter) for a proper wash.

The other problem was that, even if Annette was able to give diving and swimming exhibitions at the big swimming carnivals, publicity for this was barred from the newspapers as it was seen to be detrimental to the amateur nature of athletes.

The relative classlessness of Australia, where a convict could become a respected landowner in a few years, seemed a long way from the entrenched class system of turn-of-the-century England. Eventually it would work in her favour—Annette would become the latest amusement for the English royalty—but that was only after she had thrown herself into waters where no woman had ever swum before. For those first few weeks in England, nobody wanted to hear about an unknown Australian swimmer and her invalid dad.

The £40 the Kellermans had brought with them quickly dwindled, and Frederick and his daughter were forced to find even cheaper lodgings in the seedy Kings Cross area. Forty years later, when she was writing 'My Story', Annette vividly recalls a dingy parlour with 'the birds under glass, wax fruit and anti-macassars' as the only bright spots in the damp and dull surroundings. They managed to negotiate a ground-floor room for Frederick, who was no longer able to walk up stairs, in return for Annette agreeing to a tiny garrett with 'a slanting roof, a cot and a small broken mirror'. It had the added disadvantage of no windows and a ceiling so low that, when she stood up straight, Annette would hit her head on the roof. For the price of one guinea a week, the Kellermans had bed and a form of breakfast.

'Oh the recollections of those eggs,' Annette wrote about the meals they endured in the boarding house.

With no friends and little money they had to think fast. Fred Kellerman came up with one last chance for Annette to gain publicity. She would swim the River Thames. Even today, few attempt such a feat, but at that time the majority of people you'd come across in the river were dead—accidentally or otherwise. The section Annette and her father planned for her to swim was from Putney to Blackwall, 26 miles in all. The Putney end of the river was not too bad, but Blackwell was right in the heart of London's industrial area, and the Thames was the repository for most of its waste and sewerage.

At the end of June 1904, on a fine summer's day, Frederick Kellerman could be seen negotiating with a cockney boatman for the price of his skills and a boat to row him alongside Annette as she swam. On a diet that had mainly consisted of bread and milk, Annette dived off the wharf at Putney into the Thames.

'I shall never forget that swim through the flotsam and jetsam of London, dodging tugs and swallowing what seemed like pints of oil from the greasy surface of the river,' she wrote.

Along the way, bypassers noticed a swimmer in the river—a woman at that—and the word spread. Soon the riverbanks were lined with curious onlookers, and by the time she reached Blackwall the newspaper men had arrived. Her father was delighted, but Annette—unaware of the grease that covered her from head to toe or even what she had just achieved—had only one thought: food.

Twenty-six miles is over 42 kilometres. Even today, with an adequate diet and training, it would be an amazing feat, but back then no one had ever attempted such a thing. After weeks of bread and milk, the first thing Annette said when she climbed on to the dock was: 'I'm starving.' An old riverbank watchman gave her his lunch. 'It's only bread and cheese, miss, but you're welcome to it,' he said. Once she'd eaten the sandwich, she says she felt fighting fit again.

Waking up next morning in the tiny garret and hitting her head, yet again, on the ceiling, Annette walked downstairs and outside and was surrounded by swarms of newspaper reporters. She'd made the front pages, 'Young Australian girl swims 26 miles down the Thames', and the Kings Cross locals were out in force cheering. Her life had changed forever.

The *Daily Mirror*, the first pictorial newspaper in England, offered Annette 8 guineas a week to swim along the coast. The *Mirror* had begun just two years before in November 1903. Up until then newspapers had only offered readers illustrations of current events, but the *Daily Mirror* printed photographic images for the first time ever. It not only enlarged the readership—suddenly semi-literate people were now buying papers—but it meant that actual photographs of real events could be seen. Annette had arrived in London at just the right time. The *Mirror* gave her the chance to be documented as she swam, making her the first female athlete to benefit from this kind of publicity. As one issue stated:

> If you feel very hot this Wednesday you cannot do better than go down to Westminster baths, where Miss Kellerman—she intends to be the greatest lady swimmer of the future—introduced by the Ravensbourne club, will make her debut in an exhibition of swimming and diving. The exhibition is guaranteed to be better than a strawberry ice.

The *Mirror* christened her the 'Australian Mermaid', encouraging crowds of beachgoers to watch the young superstar swimming past. The *Daily Mirror* wanted a great deal for their money, though. For eight weeks Annette had to swim from one beach to the other all the way along the coast from Dover to Margate. Swimming five days out of seven, she would average 45 miles per week. She described it as 'the greatest training period of my entire career'. When her father worried that it might be too much for Annette—'that's a frightful lot of swimming,' he protested to the editor—he was told that if she took up the challenge, his daughter's future would be ensured: 'This will be the greatest campaign ever launched about a young girl.'

When they arrived in Dover to fulfil the *Daily Mirror*'s contract, Frederick and his daughter had a halfpenny between them. They hadn't been able to write home for some time because they couldn't afford to buy a stamp. He decided to take the finest house in town and used his considerable charm to persuade the landlady to agree to them staying. Considering no one had ever attempted what his daughter was about to do, he wasn't even really sure whether they would be able to pay.

'We bought no newspaper for a week and had to watch our chance to look over somebody's shoulder to see what the sporting man was saying about us,' Annette wrote in *How to Swim*.

It was a gruelling schedule: on Monday she was to swim from Dover to St Margaret's Bay—4 miles; on Tuesday, Dover to Deal—9 miles; on Wednesday, from Deal to Ramsgate—15 miles. Thursday was a rest day, and on Friday she would swim from Ramsgate to Margate, a distance of 10 miles. Finally on Saturday she would start out from Margate, training for an eventual Channel swim. Her father was anxious, but Annette told him not to worry: 'I never get tired,' she said.

The crowds that packed the beaches to catch a glimpse of the Australian Mermaid were so enthusiastic they had to be held back by police. Every triumph was recorded by the *Daily Mirror*. Annette was in the paper each day of the week, her picture everywhere. She was not so much a star as a phenomenon. At the end of the eight weeks, the *Mirror*'s editor stated that he was 'very anxious for her to attack the man's record from Dover to Margate, a distance of 24 miles'.

Annette was paced by Jabez Wolffe, another Channel swimming hopeful. She broke all the records ever made over this distance, and also broke the record for the size of the crowd lining the beach and cliffs at Margate waiting for her arrival.

The exposure Annette was given by the *Daily Mirror* meant that all the doors that had been closed were now opened wide. Managers were begging her to come and perform in every swimming club in England. She had also become quite adept at dealing with the press, a skill which she would perfect in her later years on the American vaudeville circuit. The journalists and Annette formed a mutual admiration society: they reported her every stunt and she kept on coming up with more. She only let them down once during this period—when she told them she ate no red meat. As she wrote in her memoirs, 'it was a staggering blow' to them to think that her 'tremendous endurance' was not down to juicy steaks, but a few measly vegetables.

One of the clubs which had opened its door to Annette was the Bath Club. If floating on their back in the ornately tiled pool, a swimmer could see the sky through a glass conservatory roof suspended on wrought iron pillars. The foyer, resplendent with exotic decorations in marble, was inspired by the intricate designs of Byzantine culture. The most exclusive club in London catered for royalty and a very few hand-picked socialites. Annette was asked to perform before the Duke and Duchess of Connaught. However, when it became known, on the day of her scheduled performance, that she swam in a man's bathing suit with her legs bare, a representative from the Bath Club was despatched immediately to speak to Annette and her father.

'You understand that you can't possibly appear before their Royal Highnesses exhibiting bare limbs,' he said.

Although she tried to explain that this was what everyone wore in Australia, the palace representative wouldn't hear of it. Annette, unfazed, decided the solution was simple: she'd wear stockings. She jumped into her bathing suit, pulled on a pair of stockings and paraded the effect before her father. There was a big gap of white flesh between the tops of her stockings and the bathing costume.

'Oh dear, no. That will never do,' said Kellerman, who was meticulous in his attire.

Annette saw the possibilities of this new suit, despite the gap. She found the longest pair of stockings she could buy and sewed them on to her bathing suit. The effect was extraordinary—the black, body-hugging suit showed every curve of her svelte, athletic body. Annette, describing herself as usual in the third person, wrote, 'The entire length of the black costume from the neck to the feet accentuated the symmetry of the figure that was to become the most famous in all the world.' The one-piece bathing suit was a success that night at the Bath Club and it became her trademark from then on.

Annette was only nineteen years old, but after eight weeks on the front page of the *Daily Mirror* she was one of the most well-known women in England. Faraway places and people were calling for her to come and swim for them, and Annette, always ready to take a challenge, was rearing to go.

3
I NEVER GET TIRED AND I SWIM LIKE A CLOCK

Reporters from the famous *Paris Match* sporting journal, standing alongside the Seine with thousands of others in September 1905, would have seen some of the most famous swimming figures of the day. The *Match* was sponsoring the annual swim along the river: the reporters were about to witness seventeen men swim for 24 miles under the seven bridges of Paris. There was one big difference this year. The difference was *une femme*, a certain Mademoiselle Annette Kellerman, who was to compete against the men. As the swimmers lined up on the starting blocks, the men—especially the Englishman Thomas Burgess—towered over Mademoiselle Kellerman, a petite 5 feet, 4 inches. She didn't look as if she could swim 12 yards, let alone 12 miles, but that wasn't the point. Just the fact that she was standing there in her man's bathing suit ready to take on the might of seventeen men meant all eyes were on her. And then, of course, it wasn't often— well never, really, outside the *Follies Bergere*—that they would have been granted the chance to see such a very shapely lady with so very little on.

For Annette, swimming down the Seine was a much more exciting experience than swimming the Thames. She'd made that attempt in desperation to gain any sort of attention she could; but here, in Paris, the home of her mother, she was welcomed like a long-lost daughter. This swim, like the Thames, ran right through the heart of the city, and again competitors had to battle not only the distance, but also the industrial pollution that poured straight into the river from industry.

When the gun went off and Annette dived in with the rest, a huge roar went up from the crowd: 'Allez Miss!', 'Go Miss, go!' The cheers continued as she swam. Each time she passed under one of the bridges, onlookers threw flowers and cheered her on. As the swimmers went further up the river, they started dropping out of the race. Annette remembers the French race referees coming by in motor boats, shouting through megaphones as they sped up and down the line of swimmers: 'only ten entrants left in the race' then, a little further on, 'only six'.

The excitement grew as the number of swimmers fell to four, with Annette still holding third place. After training along the English coast all summer, Annette was feeling strong and relaxed as she swam. When the official boat came alongside her and called out '2 kilometres, only 2 more kilometres!' Annette was easily able to increase her pace and overtake the man in second place. She gave those last 2 kilometres everything. As she approached what she thought was the final bridge, she was exuberant. When she lifted her head to take each breath, her eyes searched the river for the finishing line but she couldn't see it. At this moment, the referees' boat came alongside and they told her she had two more kilometres to go. She couldn't believe it. Later she found out that the French officials, seeing thirteen men drop out, were worried that their finest woman swimmer wouldn't make it. They thought if they told her she was almost there and egged her along for the last 2 kilometres she would finish and the race would be a success. At the time, all she felt was rage and exhaustion. She called it a 'dirty trick' and stopped then and there in the middle of the river and burst into tears. Her father, miserable in the boat beside her, caught his daughter's eye and tried to smile encouragingly. When she caught sight of her father's deathly pale face Annette burst into tears again. She was sure he was going to have a heart attack and it was all because of her; she'd let him down. Thomas Burgess, the Englishman, swam along beside her when she had almost given up.

'Well now, little girl, what's the matter?' he asked her in a thick Yorkshire accent.

With that, Annette burst into tears yet again and was only able to blurt out between sobs: 'They cheated me! They cheated me! I don't know how I can finish, I went all out on the last kilometre.'

'Come on, we'll finish it together.'

Burgess paced her for the last 2 kilometres. She believed he gave up his chance to win just for her. A hundred and eighty metres out from the finishing line, Burgess called out: 'Let's race for it!'

Incredibly, Annette found enough energy to sprint to the finish. They touched the tape together. When she emerged from the water the crowd went crazy. Burgess, who had come equal third with Annette, was virtually ignored but was to have his day when he became the second person to swim the English Channel after Captain Webb. It would be his thirteenth attempt, swum in 22 hours and 35 minutes.

That summer of 1905 in Paris belonged to Annette. It seemed the entire city had fallen in love with Mademoiselle Kellerman.

As she was leaving with her father after the race, Annette found that a crowd had surrounded a cab waiting to take them back to their hotel. A group of young men had unhitched the horse and hitched themselves up instead, pulling Fred and his daughter through the streets of Paris. She had conquered the hearts of the Parisians, and the next day she was front-page news. She wrote later: 'The French newspapers of course gave me banner headlines, but not one of them forgot to mention the fact that I was the daughter of a French Woman.' It also helped that she spoke French 'like a native' and charmed all the reporters.

There's a certain naiveté in Annette's reminiscences about this time. She ignores the fact that the media interest in her had a lot to do with what she was—or, more to the point, wasn't— wearing when she swam. The picture she paints is that she was young and proud of the body she had created through endless hard work, and she wanted to show it off. Her memoirs have the jolly optimism of a Girls' Own adventure story and, like the heroines of those stories, Annette, pure as a white rose, exudes not one whiff of awareness of the potency of her sexuality. Arguably, at the time, no one actually spoke about a woman's body in that way—it was 'athletic' or 'artistic', but not sexual. She was 'well brought up' in a very middle-class family and, until she was at least 21, constantly chaperoned by her father.

Triumph succeeded triumph when Annette descended from her man-drawn carriage at the hotel to receive telegrams from two of her mother's oldest friends, Cecile Chaminard and Nellie Mitchell, now Nellie Melba—another Australian who was setting hearts on fire in Paris with her performances at the Paris Opera.

For the next week, Annette was the talk of the town. Skits about her appeared in stage reviews, and a famous French couturier made a replica of her swimming costume and put it in the window of his salon with the caption: 'Will women ever wear this bathing suit?' Cartoonists had a field day comparing her man's bathing suit with the full regalia of the chic French women's voluminous swimwear.

Her fame spread throughout Europe. In Austria, Baroness Isa Cescu, a famous Viennese swimmer, decided she could beat the Australian. She challenged Annette to race her down the Danube from Tuln to Vienna, a distance of 22 miles. Annette accepted, and nearly killed herself in the notoriously treacherous and icy waters of the Danube. It wasn't the distance that would prove the problem, this was a race that would be won by knowing the river. The Baroness knew it well and she knew she had the advantage, insisting they start well away from each other so Annette would have to find her own way.

'I had not gone far before I found myself sucked into a shallow whirlpool,' Annette wrote. 'The water was only about 6 inches deep and was whirling around with great force and speed over a bed of sharp pebbles. Before I could work my way out my legs were one mass of cuts and bruises.'

Despite this, Annette beat the Baroness by an almost embarrassing three-quarters of an hour.

Returning to London in 1905 she was at the height of her swimming powers. It seemed there was nothing she couldn't do. Yet it was here, she wrote later, that she 'finally met her Waterloo'—the English Channel. The Channel is 22 miles wide at its narrowest point between Shakespeare beach at Dover and Cap Griz Nez, but most of those who make the Channel crossing actually swim between 30 and 40 miles because of notoriously treacherous currents and tides, which push swimmers from side to side.

At the turn of the twentieth century, the Victorian age was over but the Queen's subjects lived in an empire conquered by the adventurous. There were no new lands to be discovered, but the Channel offered the kind of challenge an Englishman loved— it was the Everest of swimming.

For Annette, it was not just the challenge but the money. Though she was extremely well known, she was still not earning much. As she joked later in *How to Swim*: 'English society was not going in for mermaids enough to keep the wolf in his den.'

The cross-Channel swim, organised by the *Daily Mirror*, was to be the culmination of Annette's series of coastal swims. The paper had sponsored a swimmer in a Channel race the year before and realised the potential of such an event. The sports editor offered to pay Annette so much for the first three hours and from then on more for each subsequent hour swimming the Channel.

'I don't want you making a fool of me or my paper,' he told her. 'I just want you to stop in the water a long enough time to justify my confidence in you.'

Annette didn't intend to 'stop in the water' at all; she was going to get to the other side. When her father expressed concern about the dangers involved, she told him: 'I never seem to get tired and you've always told me I swim like a clock.'

The race was to honour the anniversary of Captain Matthew Webb, who had swum the Channel 30 years before. The first and only person ever to have swum the Channel at that time, Webb had dived in at Admiralty Pier and eventually landed at Calais 21 hours, 44 minutes and 55 seconds later, swimming breaststroke and sipping brandy along the way. He became a national hero, always in search of greater challenges—a search which ended when he died in an ill-fated attempt to swim Niagara Falls in 1883.

Since Webb, many swimmers had tried to cross but all had failed. This may have been because the Channel, calm in the morning, could end up with gale force winds and 10 foot waves on the same afternoon. Drifting seaweed masses, shoals of mackerel (one swimmer's support team as recently as 1969 caught 182 large mackerel as they accompanied him across), jellyfish, Portuguese men-of-war and 15 foot sharks could also be encountered. The currents were unpredictable and the water an icy sixteen degrees Centigrade. None of this seems to have daunted Channel contenders. The insurmountable odds seemed to spur them on. Between 1898 and 1911, when Thomas Burgess made the next successful crossing after Webb, over 72 unsuccessful Channel attempts were made.

Perhaps the most unlucky swimmer of them all, or the most optimistic, was the Glasgow native Jabez Wolffe, who failed in every one of his 22 attempts. In 1911 it was by mere yards, and by only a mile on three other occasions. Wolffe tried a series of different strategies to get himself across, including being accompanied by Pipe Major Nicholls, who played the bagpipes to keep Wolffe's stroke in rhythm. He reasoned that if music could make men march, it might also help them to swim. At other times, when the Major was out on manoeuvres, he used a gramophone aboard the pilot boat to achieve the same ends. Annette, who would meet him in her first Channel swim, described him in How to Swim as 'pretty fat for athletic work and [he] would hardly make a distinguished showing in any other event', but acknowledged he was a very good swimmer.

The 1905 Webb Memorial Channel Race had five contestants including the Yorkshireman Burgess and the unfortunate Wolffe. Annette was the only woman. The lead-up to the race was recorded in the paper every day. The swimmers trained constantly.

One day, a couple of weeks before the race, Annette and Burgess actually ran into each other in the sea: 'Lady and gentleman stood up, treading water twenty fathoms deep and shook hands,' said the *Daily Mirror*. Both wished each other luck. As she swam off in the other direction, Burgess had a chance to surreptitiously size up the competition. He remarked how, without seeming to make an effort, 'she forges through the water. She is the most disciplined swimmer I have ever seen.' Annette was still using the double-armed trudgeon. It was first learned by Englishman John Trudgeon from South American Indians, in 1875.

Annette took her swimming seriously, almost scientifically. Later, in her manual *How to Swim*, she gives glimpses of the sort of determination it took for her to reach the point of swimming the English Channel: 'Though it may seem paradoxical one must have absolute abandon and at the same time minute precision to become a good swimmer.' She advises her readers that to strengthen the legs or upper body they must swim with hands or feet tied together. Her record for swimming with her arms tied behind her back is an amazing 1 ½ miles.

Her swimming prowess, and in particular her 'pluck', were the inspiration for many news stories at the time. In a trial Channel swim in July 1905, the *Daily Mirror* reported:

> She started with a powerful double-armed stroke and soon made considerable progress at 46 strokes to the minute. There was a big swell on and now the plucky swimmer would appear far above the boat poised on the crest of a wave, the next moment she would be lost to sight in the deep trough of green sea. After swimming twenty minutes Miss Kellerman called for chocolate. Whilst taking this she kept on her way with a powerful sidestroke. Soon, however, she began to complain of

seasickness but pluckily refused to come out of the water. By a quarter past eleven . . . the sea was getting still rougher but the plucky lady refused to give in.

'I feel strong and warm,' she said, 'but this horrible feeling is growing worse.' However after an hour's swim, having covered four miles, Miss Kellerman was persuaded to enter the boat. It was a most noteworthy exhibition of pluck and she almost broke down at having to give in.

It seems her lashings of pluck were no match for the lashings of Cadbury's Bourneville Cocoa she consumed before, during and after the swim. The *Daily Mirror* was not the only sponsor Annette had for the Channel swim. Photos published in the *Mirror* show her sipping away at the cocoa and landing after the trial swim, where she endorses the product that had made her so sick: 'I find it more nourishing and sustaining than any other I have tried before,' is the caption on a full-page photo of the 'great swimmer'. Later, she would advise chicken broth sipped from a bottle as a much better alternative for a Channel swim: 'stick to foods that stick to you'.

The race was set for 25 August 1905. Though it was high summer, the water temperature would have been between only 53 and 60 degrees Fahrenheit, or about 15–16 degrees Centigrade.

'No fewer than five plucky aspirants for the honour of equalling Captain Webb's great feat started on their tremendous task,' reported the *Daily Mirror*. The five were Annette, Thomas Burgess, Motague Holbien, Horace Pew and Jabez Wolffe. The men were allowed to swim naked, covered with seal fat, but Annette had to wear a swimming costume, which chaffed her badly under the arms. All started from different locations 1 mile apart because each swimmer, having studied the coast and tides like a gambler studies the form guide, had decided on the most advantageous place. Just as Webb had done before her, Annette, covered in porpoise oil and with her goggles glued on tightly, dived in off Admiralty Pier and straight into the Channel.

'You start out absolutely alone,' Annette wrote later, 'No one is allowed to give you the slightest assistance. If you so much as touch the boat or rest your fingers on the oar you are "declared out".'

Like the other swimmers, she was accompanied by a steam tug and a row boat. The idea was that the tug would stay a few hundred yards away and protect her from high seas. Every half hour she would swim alongside the big boat and be given a beaker to drink from or be handed a sandwich on the end of a long stick.

The first few hours went well, with the *Daily Mirror* reporter covering the event from the support boat. For the first hour or so, Annette was accompanied in the water by an admirer, a certain Tom Reese, a well known billiard player and a fine swimmer, who was in a playful mood.

'I'll propose to you,' he cried.

'And I'll accept,' laughed back the cheery swimmer.

'Oh no,' shouted Mr Kellerman from the accompanying tug. 'I can't allow that. She's too young to marry.'

When the westward tide turned there were no more jokes. It made progress slow, almost pushing Annette backwards. It also made the sea very choppy and again the Cadbury's cocoa caused her trouble.

'A manufacturer had supplied me with a good deal of cocoa . . . but after four hours the chocolate and the chop of the water made me very seasick and from then on for the rest of the swim I was seasick every half hour,' Annette wrote in *How to Swim*.

She had been in the water more than six hours and refused to give up, saying over and over: 'The longer you stick, the more you get.' Eventually her father and the boat men had to drag her out very unwillingly.

None of the contenders succeeded the swim on this occasion. Annette made two more attempts to cross the English Channel. On the last she could clearly see the French coastline, but rough seas and seasickness prevented her from landing. Her record of $10\frac{1}{2}$ hours in the water held until Gertrude Ederhle broke it in 1926, when she became the first woman to swim the Channel.

Annette believed she had the endurance required, but not the brute strength to go with it. 'I think no woman has this combination: that's why I say that none of my sex will ever accomplish that particular stunt.' It sounds like sour grapes, but it must be remembered that, at the time, it had been 30 years since anyone had come near to crossing the Channel. Burgess didn't make it across for another six years and Ederhle didn't succeed until 21 years later. The training methods and knowledge of diet were also still very primitive and, after all, she was the most remarkable female swimmer of her day. It seemed perfectly logical—if she couldn't do it, who could?

The third attempt on the Channel was her last. She had other engagements. In between training and attempts to cross the Channel, Annette was supporting herself and her father by giving swimming and diving demonstrations in indoor pools all over London. At that time, it was an occupation that could be surprisingly dangerous. And unfortunately Frederick was suffering more and more angina attacks, so could no longer take his daughter to the swimming galas or make sure the conditions were right for her.

Annette's diving skills were the selling point of these demonstrations. Diving had only recently been introduced into England by the Swedes who had been developing diving since the beginning of the nineteenth century. The impact was amazing—audiences were still unable to believe how a diver could fly through the air so gracefully. Because diving was still such a novelty in England at this time there were not really any true diving boards. Annette had to leap from very primitive, hastily constructed planks, nothing like springboards today. On one particular night she was performing at a pool where they had just tacked a board on to a balcony for her performance. And no one told her the pool was shallow.

Annette did a one and a half dive and smashed head first into the hard, tiled surface of the bottom of the pool. When she floated to the surface blood was streaming down her face. The audience gasped and two bath attendants dived in to pull her out. She lost consciousness for some minutes. Her first question when she came to was: 'Will I be able to dive again soon?' When they took her to hospital to give her six stitches, she worried more about her father than herself. She knew he always waited anxiously for her after the show so she begged the doctor to allow her to return home as soon as possible and then played down the whole thing, telling her father she'd be able to work again very soon. She couldn't afford not to. By now she was supporting not only her ailing father, but her family back in Australia.

Annette had signed a contract to perform at big swimming galas for between three and five guineas a week, and went back into the very unhygienic indoor pools too early, before her forehead had properly healed and despite her doctor's warnings. Her wound became badly infected and had to be drained. With no antibiotics to stem the infection she almost died.

'You will bear a scar for the rest of your life down the front of your forehead,' the doctor told her.

'Oh well, I will just wear my hair down the front, that's all,' she replied.

And she did. In all her photos she had a fringe and a scarf over her forehead. In all her writings, Annette never mentioned it again. She was not vain about her face, only taking pride in her body. This was just one of the many life-threatening accidents Annette was to survive during her career, and she always did so with the same fearless optimism. Like the heroine in her Girls' Own adventure tale, she took the consequences for what she did, but never let anything daunt her for long. Within a week, she was hired by Arthur Collins to perform at the London Hippodrome, scarred forehead and all.

Described as 'one of the most remarkable buildings in this great city', the Hippodrome was one of London's premier variety theatres. The music hall or variety tradition began with the entertainment in local inns of the sixteenth century, and then moved on to bigger venues. By the time Annette arrived in London, there were four different levels of theatrical experience—first, the aristocratic variety theatre of the West End, chiefly found in the immediate neighbourhood of Leicester Square; then the smaller and less aristocratic West End halls; next, the large bourgeois music halls of the less fashionable suburbs; and last, the minor music halls of the poor and squalid districts. A description from *Harper's New Monthly Magazine* of January 1891 gives some idea of the scale of the Hippodrome:

Its exterior is more handsome and imposing than that of most London theatres, even of the highest rank. Huge cressets in classical tripods flare between the columns of the façade, the windows and foyer glow with stained glass, the entrance hall, lighted by softened electric lamps, is richly and tastefully decorated. You pass through wide, airy corridors and down stairs, to find yourself in a magnificent theatre, and the stall to which you are shown is wide and luxuriously fitted. Smoking is universal, and a large proportion of the audience promenade the outer circles, or stand in groups before the long refreshment bars which are a prominent feature on every tier. Most of the men are in evening dress, and in the boxes are some ladies, also in evening costume, many of them belonging to what is called good society. The women in the other parts of the house are generally pretty obvious members of a class which, so long as it behaves itself with propriety in the building, it would, whatever fanatics may say to the contrary, be neither desirable nor possible to exclude. There is a large and excellent orchestra, with just a tendency to overdo the drum and cymbals. Stage footmen, more gorgeous of livery but far meeker of aspect than their brethren in private service, slip a giant card bearing a number into a gilded frame on either side of the proscenium before each item of the programme. The electric bell tings, the lights are raised, the orchestra dashes into a prelude, and the artiste whose 'turn' it is comes on.

The Hippodrome specialised in equestrian, gymnastic and menagerie 'turns' until the last act, which traditionally had to have at least one aquatic scene of one sort, suiting Annette perfectly. She performed in what was described at the time as a large tank, or 'lake which by a wonderful mechanical process, when required, fills up the circus ring'. The Hippodrome audiences were to Annette's taste as well—unlike those in other variety venues, they were not of 'the lounging after dinner or "round the town" kind, but are in a great measure formed of family groups, headed by pater or mater, or both. Indeed, most of its patrons are of the sedate domestic sort.' This was due to the fact that there was no liquor licence, as in other theatres, so people felt it was safe to bring young children and women along. Here Annette could do more than just demonstrate diving and swimming. She and her father felt in no way inferior because they were Australians in the heart of London. In fact, being an Antipodean mermaid gave Annette much of her mystique. Her show at the Hippodrome was a celebration of her Australianness. As she dived from the high board, she would give a loud 'coo-ee' and emerge wet and smiling to rapturous applause. Any Australians in the audience would 'coo-ee' back. She was not yet twenty, young, beautiful, brave and nearly naked a lot of the time. Usually-reticent male Londoners, their mouths agape in admiration, gushed over the little Australian mermaid: 'To the Coo-ee Girl, have never seen her like and perhaps never shall again and nor do I want to,' wrote one fan, Victor M. Mansil. Sir George Alexander, the famous actor manager, wrote in Annette's autograph book: 'The stars should be your pearls on a string, the world a ruby for your finger. And you should have the sun and moon to wear if I were King.'

On the night of her hundredth show at the Hippodrome, Annette gave her usual coo-ee to the audience and received a lusty reply in the form of a Maori war cry from the appreciative New Zealand football team. The reviewer from *The London Spectator* was there that night and was obviously another big fan:

There is that in Miss Kellerman's display that causes one to regret when her all too rapid twelve minutes in the Hippodrome tank are ended and arouses a desire to witness it again. The 'mermaid' compels attention . . . she laughs and talks, brings fish out of the water as if she had caught them and intimates to those in the front that she is an Australian girl, with the bushman's cry of 'Coo-ee'. At the end of the night Miss Kellerman just nods to the audience as if to say 'Good Night' and goes away.

Annette took all this admiration in her stride, but was bowled over when Queen Alexandra requested Annette be presented to her. She remembers in 'My Story':

Shaking at the knees and trembling with excitement, I was ushered in to Her Majesty, the Queen of England. What a picture came to view—the Queen was sitting in an armchair calmly nursing a baby tiger, the small animal having just been born at the Hippodrome.

Annette much preferred performing in a theatre than in swimming baths because she felt closer to achieving her desire to become an actress. Even though she was still performing aquatic tricks in a glass tank, she was at least in a legitimate theatre. There were other reasons why she took to the theatre rather than staying in the pools and the most pressing one was a young Australian swimmer called Beatrice Kerr. She had arrived in England just two years after Annette, and was following just a little too closely in her footsteps. However, Beatrice wasn't happy just to follow; she was keen to overtake. Twice she issued a challenge to Annette to race her over 100 yards and twice Annette refused to take the bait. It was a wise move on Annette and Frederick's part because Beatrice could indeed swim faster over the distance. She realised that if she beat Annette it would make her famous: 'I shall be unhappy till I meet her,' Beatrice told reporters on more than one occasion, 'because people won't believe till then that I am so good a swimmer as she.'

Beatrice enjoyed considerable popularity in London, particularly with her 'Monte Carlo Bag Trick', where she would climb into a canvas bag doused in petrol at the top of the diving platform and set it alight. The audience saw a ball of fire drop into the water and Beatrice would emerge unscathed, having discarded the bag underwater. But the fame didn't last. She returned home to Sydney and lived a quiet life in the beachside suburb of Coogee. Beatrice never met her rival though they were in the same city for more than a year. Beatrice remained in London while Annette moved on. Her season at the London Hippodrome had ended. America was beckoning and Annette, ready for new adventures, was answering the call.

4
CARNIVAL TIME

The telegram was addressed to her, so Annette opened it. 'Will you appear at White City Amusement Park, Chicago?' it read.

'Will I?' she thought, 'America, my word I will!' She ran in to tell her father the good news. He was dozing in an armchair and looked very pale and worn.

She wrote later in her memoirs that she had wondered whether he would be able to stand the excitement of the trip and the happenings in a new land. She just couldn't tell him. Just then, Frederick opened his eyes and, seeing the telegram, asked what it was about. Trying to keep calm, but barely able to control her excitement, Annette blurted out the contents. To her relief, he was just as excited.

'Of course we'll go,' he told her. 'Our worries are at an end. It's the land of opportunity!'

Neither had any idea exactly what White City Amusement Park was, and only a general idea of the geographical location of the city of Chicago. But it didn't matter. They were sailing to America, second class, on a White Star liner.

White City Amusement Park had opened a year before, in 1906. It was one of many such parks opening all over the country. The forerunners of the theme parks of today, and every bit as lavish, these parks often had the same standardised amusements—White City's 'Fighting Flames Fire Show', which thrilled park-goers with a realistically staged hotel inferno, was almost identical to the fire show at 'Wonderland' in Revere Beach where Annette went to work after White City. The outdoor set depicted a life-sized city block and required the use of two trolley cars, five cabs, two automobiles, several fire-fighting wagons, fourteen horses and 250 actors; it was an excellent drawcard at both parks. Also very popular was the 'Canals of Venice', a 'romantic gondola ride through the moonlit water streets of Venice' where patrons could view 'correct reproductions' of the city's 'famous buildings and statuary groups'.

In 1906, Chicago was smack bang in the middle of the Jazz Age. Social mores had changed dramatically in the past five to ten years, especially for young people—for the first time they were going out alone, and had the chance to meet people and fall in love.

Amusement parks were places specifically designed to accommodate the new freedom of white middle-class youths, and White City purported to be a good, wholesome place packed with nice clean fun. But some Chicagoans believed the park to be not without its temptations. The 'Casino' dance hall sold alcohol freely to its mainly teenage patrons, and much of the music was played by all-Black jazz bands such as the Charles Elgar and Charles Cook bands, which would have heightened racist observers' suspicions about the 'wholesomeness' of White City. Entertainments which would be highly questionable today, like Midget City, a 'model miniature village of twenty-five tiny buildings peopled by a host of midgets of world-wide renown', and the 'Infant Incubators', where premature babies were put on display, were considered amusing and even a little enlightening.

After the stuffy formalities of London life, Chicago was crass and loud, modern and exciting. When Annette and her father stepped off the boat, they landed right in the thick of it all and, quite unprepared, were immediately surrounded by reporters.

'The press, so unlike the conservative English press, were there en masse,' wrote Annette. 'But opening the papers the next morning I found all sorts of stories about my exploits and life. I turned to my dad and said "but most of these things have never happened to me at all".'

The Kellermans had managed to get what Annette described as a 'little enclosure on the principal thoroughfare—right across the road from the "Iggerotes" and next door to the snake man!' The place had a high false front, but no roof. They had a specially built tank only 14 feet long and 5½ feet deep, which was very shallow for swimming, let alone diving. The tank was surrounded by seats, 'like in a circus'.

'I gave three examples of the most approved styles of swimming, did some fantastic stunts—porpoise swimming and the like—and sixteen dives, backward, forward and sidewise. At last I was making good money steadily,' Annette wrote in *How to Swim*.

Annette won the press over by turning her first show, which could have been a disaster, into a triumph. Though it was the end of May, the day she opened snow began to fall just as the reporters arrived, bundled up in raincoats. She described the performance in 'My Story':

> They took it for granted that they had come on a wild goose chase but I said 'No—you've come all the way to White City Park to see me—I'll do the best I can for you'. And, with the reporters seated in the front rows, with snow coming down in big flakes, I gave my first show in the United States.

One of the people who was there that first day was a young man named James R. Sullivan, a program seller at the park. He wrote later: 'I was passing a concession in White City Park and I was attracted by the sign 'Australian Mermaid'. I noticed a number of men passing in through the gate with their overcoat collars turned up. It was snowing and I couldn't help wondering what was going on. I followed. Imagine my surprise when I saw them all take their place around a diving pool. A few minutes later a figure in a bathrobe mounted the steps to the diving board. Through the snowflakes I could see a black-clad figure move to the end of the board and then dive into the pool. As this was supposed to be summer there were no heating arrangements. I'll say one thing, those reporters saw a show and enjoyed it cold or no cold.'

When James R. Sullivan met the Kellermans he wondered how such obviously well-educated middle-class people had ended up working in an amusement park. As he got to know them better he realised that they never put on superior airs and graces but 'just took everything in their stride'. Both were extremely popular with the show people, with Annette in particular being a favourite with everyone in the park. Whatever she was doing and whoever she was with, Jimmie wrote in his memoir of life with Annette, 'she remained her own cheery self'.

When a letter arrived from Alice Kellerman saying she would like to move the family back to Paris, Frederick, now confined to a wheelchair, confided to Annette that they probably wouldn't have enough money to help this year.

Annette told her father that she'd just do a few more shows and they'd get them there in no time. She decided to peform 55 shows a week—five or six a day on weekdays and between twelve and eighteen on weekends. 'It's nothing to swimming 50 miles a week,' she told her father.

One Sunday, when Annette had completed her eighteenth show and was standing outside her concession discussing business with Jimmie, she met John L. Sullivan, the famous boxer, who asked her how many shows she'd done that day. She wrote later that when she told him, he replied: 'Jehosophat! You can stay the rounds too eh?'

After that first show in the snow Annette had rave reviews, and crowds queued outside the little enclosure to see the 'Australian Mermaid'. But the strain was telling on Fred Kellerman, and he was finding it difficult to keep up. As he came to know and trust Jimmie, a friendship soon grew between the men. He began to rely more and more on the younger man for support. Soon Jimmie was working for the Kellermans as Fred's assistant manager and press agent. At first, especially in Chicago, Annette didn't see much of Jimmie—and when she did, it was usually to ask him a favour.

Because he was so busy managing Annette, Fred had asked his sister Josephine to come and stay with them and be a chaperone to Annette, whom he couldn't keep an eye on all the time and who was, for obvious reasons, very popular with the boys.

Aunt Josephine turned out to be a very strict chaperone—for Annette, used to having her way in most things, much too strict. She certainly didn't want her aunt around all the time. So she enlisted Jimmie, who seemed 'very kind'.

'He rendered me all kinds of services and, above all, helped me with my little flirtations with the boys,' she later wrote about him.

At the time, Annette, never one to sit around twiddling her thumbs between shows, was learning to play golf with one of her admirers. Jimmie was left to persuade Aunt Josephine that, while she was in Chicago, she should really see some of the wonderful sites that city possessed. He took her sightseeing whenever necessary (which was often), showing her 'everything from the stockyards to the museums'. Especially the museums— later he told Annette he never wanted to see another museum in his life. He also told her about his strategy for turning away the university boys who hung outside the enclosure hoping to meet Annette. She described it in 'My Story':

'How about meeting the mermaid?' they'd ask him.

'Gee fellows I can't do it,' he'd reply. 'Her dad is a big whale of an Australian and he chews up little fellows like you.'

Jimmie helped Annette with other favours. Because she was always in strict training her father severely rationed her favourite food in the United States, ice-cream. If she had had her way that would have been all she ate. Often, at the end of a long gruelling day performing, there'd be knock at her hotel room door and a package of ice-cream would be thrust through by Jimmie, who always left before she could say thankyou.

Their relationship was very much Annette as the star and Jimmie as the paid manager. When she received an offer to work at Wonderland amusement park at Revere Beach, Boston, it was Jimmie who went ahead to organise things. Her father had told her that the money she had made in Chicago had bought her mother, sister, two brothers and five dogs a house in Paris. He also told her he was going to join them.

'I have gone with you as far as I can go. But now it's time for me to be with your mother,' he said.

Annette was not ready for him to leave. She realised that she would never have done anything had it not been for her dad. Surprisingly, for a father and teenage daughter, they had got on tremendously well even though they had spent most of that time exclusively in each other's company, her father's health being the only cloud in their sunny relations. In London Annette had been particularly worried about him. She wrote in 'My Story',

> I never went to bed without worrying whether he'd be alive in the morning. At his bedside were his digitalis pills. Many were the times when I would have to crush one of those capsules and give it to him while tears of agony rained down his face. He would recuperate just as quickly and between spells it was an unwritten law that neither of us would mention the attack that had just passed.

Frederick's health had deteriorated considerably since their arrival in the United States. He had really only been waiting to see Annette safely launched on her career path and the family settled in Paris so he could go back to them—it had been three years since he'd seen them. Annette was going to miss him; she described him as 'a charming, well-educated Australian, devoted husband and father'. He had a good sense of humour and would laugh uproariously every time he opened an American newspaper. 'What superb storytellers they are over here!' he'd say.

Left: Alice Charbonnet, Annette's talented and well-connected mother. Alice was friends with such stars as Sarah Bernhardt, whose career the young Annette longed to emulate. (Mitchell Library SLNSW) **Right:** Annette's beloved father Frederick, who was instrumental in launching Annette's international career. (Mitchell Library SLNSW)

Left: Annette with her sister Marcelle and brother Maurice, dressed in outfits influenced by their mother's Gallic roots. (Courtesy Hilton Cordell Productions) **Right:** A star in the making: eight-year-old Annette displays the charm and talent that would see her become one of the most adored women of her time. (Courtesy Hilton Cordell Productions)

THE START AT JOHNSTON STREET BRIDGE.

REFRESHMENTS BY THE WAY.

MISS ANNETTE KELLERMAN'S TEN AND A QUARTER MILE SWIM, ON THE YARRA, ON TUESDAY, 11th INST.

Swimming in the Yarra at the turn of the century. Annette was already making a name for herself as a swimmer of great ability and speed. (Courtesy Hilton Cordell Productions)

Left: By the Yarra, in the kind of bathing costume that would soon be drawing the crowds to her vaudeville show in London. (Courtesy Hilton Cordell Productions) **Right:** Annette made the first of three attempts to swim the English Channel in 1905, and though unsuccessful it was big news back home in Australia. This drawing appeared in a Melbourne newspaper. (Courtesy Barbara Firth)

THE LADY CHANNEL-SWIMMER'S BEST DIVE.

'Water always teaches me a new story ...' An exuberant Annette, at around 18 years old, by her beloved ocean. (Courtesy Hilton Cordell Productions)

Picture Perfect: after a 25-year search for the woman who most closely matched the proportions of the Venus de Milo, Dr Dudley Sargent, of Harvard University, named Annette the Perfect Woman in 1908. (Courtesy Barbara Firth)

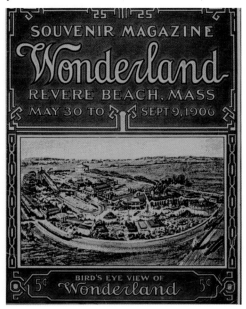

A clipping from the *Denver Times*, 1910. Annette was one of the earliest advocates of exercise for women, and was admired for her hard-earned, un-corseted curves. (Courtesy Barbara Firth)

Left: Annette was first lured to the United States in 1906 to perform at amusement parks such as Wonderland, where she gave swimming and diving exhibitions up to ten times a day. (Courtesy Hilton Cordell Productions) **Right:** Before making Hollywood films, Annette had been the highest paid female vaudeville star of her day, playing to packed houses in London and New York. (Courtesy Barbara Firth)

Neptune's Daughter, Annette's first film, was released to popular acclaim in 1914. (Courtesy Barbara Firth)

Left: Annette took up wire walking in 1916, and incorporated it into both her vaudeville act and the film *Queen of the Sea*.(Mitchell Library SLNSW) **Right:** Two years after Annette's first film came the hugely successful *A Daughter of the Gods*. It was the first Hollywood film with a million-dollar budget.(Courtesy Barbara Firth)

Annett Kellerman 1915

A passionate Herbert Brenon directs Annette on the set of *A Daughter of the Gods*. (Courtesy Hilton Cordell Productions)

Reclining in splendour for *Neptune's Daughter*. Annette openly acknowledged her face was not her best asset and often insisted on being photographed in profile. This is one of few images where she faces the camera. (Courtesy Hilton Cordell Productions)

A Daughter of the Gods gave Annette (at centre) the long-awaited chance to show off her dancing skills.
(Courtesy Hilton Cordell Productions)

Swathes of virgin Jamaican rainforest were felled to construct lavish sets like this for *A Daughter of the Gods*. Many locals were employed for the duration of filming and thousands of dollars were pumped into the local economy.
(Courtesy Hilton Cordell Productions)

Annette was brave and independent and a wonderful athlete, but it was still very much a man's world that she was trying to conquer. Now that he was leaving, Frederick had appointed a successor whom he hoped would be just as reliable, Jimmie Sullivan.

Though Annette had virtually saved the family by displaying herself in a one-piece bathing suit, Frederick had always believed implicitly she was educating as well as entertaining her audience, 'showing young women just what they could achieve in physical health through her example of exercise and diet'.

Annette continued to see herself as something of a mixture between a health crusader and an entertainer throughout her career. Indeed, she gave extremely popular lectures on physical beauty at the time she was enjoying her greatest success on the New York vaudeville circuit.

Part of Annette's popularity was due to her relaxed, natural presence on stage. Her openness and sense of security came from the support and love of her family. To start with, she hadn't been thrust into the harsh world of showbiz alone—her father was always there to look after her interests. She trusted him implicitly, and he returned that trust. Had she entered the world of amusement parks by herself, she may never have left. A young woman performing on her own at that time could easily have been seduced into the more sleazy side of park life: the itinerant life on the road moving from park to park, going nowhere.

When Annette and her father finally said goodbye at the docks on that summer's day in 1907 she had a feeling it would be the last time she would ever see him.

'He looked so small and pathetic but undaunted,' she recalled in 'My Story'.

'Remember you can rise above any conditions,' he told her. 'Never forget you were lucky to have a great artist for a mother.'

Three months later, she received a telegram from her mother telling her that Frederick had died peacefully at home. He was interred in the family grave at the famous Pere Lachaise cemetery in Paris.

5
SCANDAL IN BOSTON

Annette was now in Boston. She had missed her father's company from the minute he left and felt lonely without him. Jimmie, though he was ever thoughtful and very diligent in looking after the business side of things, was no replacement. But she did find soul mates and close friends in Pawnee Bill and his wife Miss May Lillie. One of the best known characters in the West, Pawnee was descibed in the Wonderland souvenir program of 1908 as having 'never claimed any credit for killing man or beast. His voice has always been lifted for peace'. Miss Lillie, like Annette, had come from a middle-class family. She too was strong-willed, persuading her parents to send her to college, where she obtained a Bachelor of Arts degree, but she turned her back on all that and went to live on the prairies, where the program claims she took to cattle and horses, 'as most girls gravitate to ball rooms and pink teas . . . while her classmates were making conquests of city hearts, she was roping steers and studying the art of remaining comfortable on the hurricane deck of a bucking mustang'.

Pawnee Bill's Wild West Show was the biggest act in Wonderland—including a performance by the native American

Indians, 'assisted by about two dozen cowboys and cowgirls, a troupe of Cossacks, a company of the US Cavalry and other wild riders and actors of high and low degree'. Annette had met Pawnee and Lillie when she wandered through the Indian Village after the show. They became almost like parents to her, showing some of the tricks of rough riding and telling her tales of the old West. Pawnee may have been the star attraction, but Annette wasn't far behind, drawing capacity crowds. The Wonderland program described her as:

> A clever, magnetic, beautiful, magnificently formed and modest young woman who comes nearer to being the reincarnated 'Daughter of Neptune' than any other creature. When she leaves the springboard she seems to move in space in wondrous curves and suddenly cleaves and glides into the water with the clean smoothness of a lithe oily body. No visitor to Wonderland should fail . . . to see the enchanting exhibitions of this charming young natator.

Billed as 'the largest amusement park in the world', Wonderland was on a much grander scale than White City. Set on 25 acres of prime real estate right on Revere Beach, it had been built at a cost of US$1 million, an enormous sum at the time. Annette had moved up a step in the amusement park ladder, and so had the size of her concession. Her huge billing—'ANNETTE KELLERMAN, The Australian Mermaid'— could be seen from almost everywhere in the park. It was here at Revere Beach, that she was to become infamous in the act that would lead to her discovery as the 'perfect woman' by Dr Sargent.

When she first arrived in Boston Annette headed straight to the beach. Jimmie had suggested she might do a few swims along the coast to attract publicity. She was keen as she hadn't been near the ocean since she'd arrived in America almost a year before and was curious to see an American beach. She was absolutely shocked at what she discovered. She wrote later in 'My Story':

> How could these women swim with shoes—stockings—bloomers—skirts—overdresses with puffed sleeves—sailor collars—in some cases even tightly fitted corsets? But then nobody really went swimming. Everybody waded in and out and then just bobbed up and down. Those who did swim were so heavily encumbered that they showed no joy in swimming.

The decision for Annette to swim in and around Boston in her Australian man's bathers must have been, in the light of what others were wearing, consciously made to attract attention, but neither Annette nor Jimmie knew quite how much of a scandal she would cause. According to Annette, the minute she put her foot on the beach and revealed her bare legs she elicited immediate 'ooos' and 'ahhs', and even some shrieks of terror. Crowds formed around to see what all the trouble was about. She wrote:

> Before you could say Jack Robinson, a policeman, six foot tall, appeared from nowhere. Forcing his way through the crowd, he stopped me yelling, 'hey what are you doing in that suit?'

She explained that she was about to go for a 3 mile swim out to the Boston light. The policeman told her she couldn't go anywhere in that suit. Annette was indignant: 'My word! You don't expect me to go for a 3 mile swim in a bathing costume like those over there.'

The policeman was non committal, saying only that she 'could tell it to the judge'.

Annette's account of her courtroom scene is that she stood up and did just that, telling the judge in commonsense language that swimming was the best exercise in the world and that she had been a cripple and it was swimming that had cured her. Some day, she claimed, every hospital would have a pool for those who couldn't walk. She told him that to her it seemed more criminal for women to be wearing all those clothes in the water. For one thing, they had more chance of drowning and for another they would never learn to swim. What she wore in the water made much more sense.

Luckily for Annette, the judge was good natured. He allowed Annette to wear the bathing suit, but only on the condition that she kept it concealed underneath a robe until she entered the water. The program for her show at Wonderland now boasted a photo of Annette in her robe at Revere Beach with the quote 'when the robe came off the police moved in'.

In almost every way the court case was a success for Annette. She was able to disseminate her views on swimming and health and, from the interest her opinions aroused in the press, she was able to design the first modern bathing suit for women. It was simple and straightforward, like her philosophy. She placed a tight-fitting knit jersey skirt that came down to just above the knees over her existing bathing suit. It was an early form of the modesty panel that was to exist in women's bathing suits right up to the 1960s. Annette knew exactly what she was doing, and the modesty panel worked like a charm—the first time she was wore the suit at Revere Beach women rushed up, not to vilify her but to ask her where they could buy one.

It was at this time that Doctor Sargent made his pronouncement and the Australian Mermaid became the Perfect Woman.

Annette, who remained remarkably unpretentious in many ways, even at the height of her fame, found the title a rather double-edged sword. As she wrote:

> Being the perfect woman antagonises other women. You can't be superior with them. You must be on their plane. They don't like to think you're flaunting your perfections at them. That's why I'm glad the Lord gave me a homely face . . . and a saving sense of humour . . . so I can laugh at my . . . face.

Though she was able to joke about the title, she felt a certain responsibility to remain as physically perfect as possible for her fans. She kept her image squeaky clean—no drinking, smoking or meat-eating, and massive amounts of exercise. She was an active person, unable to sit still, so at this stage it didn't bother her, but as she aged she kept up an almost obsessive exercise routine. As a star who was photographed constantly, she wasn't always as free from vanity as she made out—well into her eighties she would only allow photographs to be taken when she was fully made up, and then only from certain angles.

The idea of the perfect woman in 1908 was vastly different from what it would be today. Professor Sargent's ideal woman had to have the classic proportions of the Venus de Milo. Annette's measurements, as numerous graphs and comparisons testified, were remarkably similar to this ideal of classical perfection. The Greeks obviously preferred a fuller figured woman, and photographs of Annette at the time show a surprisingly voluptuous shape for such an accomplished athlete. Annette was slightly smaller than Venus all over with the exception of an extra three-quarters of an inch in height—and also had the advantage of a pair of fully functioning forearms.

	Kellerman	Venus
Height	5ft 4¾ in	5ft 4 in
Neck	12.6 in	14.8 in
Waist	26.2 in	31.2 in
Shoulders	37.8 in	40 in
Upper Arms	12 in	13.3 in
Fore Arm	9.4 in	
Chest	33.4 in	34 in
Foot length	9 in	10.4 in
Weight	128 lbs	130 lbs

When Jimmie took over as manager and press agent in Boston, the coverage Annette received was far wider and more stage-managed than when she was with her father. Jimmie was a very canny agent, and when Annette complained of the ridiculous things journalists wrote about her, he told her that in the United States the press was paramount and to have any publicity at all, let alone as much as she had, was to be very lucky indeed. Most of the time the coverage was good, though not always.

After her father left, she and Aunt Josephine had found a suite of three rooms in what seemed to be a respectable Boston boarding house. Mr and Mrs Pattee were their hosts. Unfortunately, Mrs Pattee, though kind at first, was unable to tolerate the Perfect Woman in the vicinity of her husband. She named Annette as a co-respondant in their subsequent divorce. The *Philadelphia Herald* reported:

Mrs Pattee's complaint averred that Pattee used to sit for hours in the kitchen of their home at Revere Beach drinking beer and eating crackers with Miss K. and alleged further that her husband had insisted that Miss K. should live in the same house with them in Boston . . . 'This is a shameful and wicked thing to say such things about me,' said Miss K . . . tears streaming down her face. 'I hardly knew Mr Pattee, I never liked him, even as a passing acquaintance . . . Mrs Pattee was very friendly to me but I hardly saw Mr Pattee. I would meet him occasionally but only exchange the most ordinary greetings with him. I never sat in the kitchen with him, I never drank beer with him. I haven't tasted a glass of beer since I have been in this country. I could not do it and keep up with my work. I finally became so disgusted with the squabbling of the Pattees that I moved . . . Wherever I go I'm always particular to be chaperoned. It is a shame and a wicked and terrible lie to try to drag my name into the divorce courts.'

However, fame wasn't all bad. A big-time producer heard about her and came down to Boston in search of the Australian Mermaid. When B.F. Keith finally found Annette's concession at Wonderland, she almost missed out on the career move of her life.

Keith had started in Boston in the early 1880s with just one vaudeville theatre, and had gradually begun taking over more and more of them all over the country. He went into partnership with Edward Albee, who was the paternal grandfather of the playwright of the same name, adopted and named after him by Albee's son Reese and wife Francis when he was two weeks old. Albee senior was a very good businessman, and together he and Keith created the Keith circuit, which came to have a virtual monopoly on the American vaudeville circuit. They owned the majority of theatres in the country.

Unfortunately, on the day Keith came to find Annette he first had to pass through the eagle eyes of Jimmie, who'd had a particularly difficult day fending off Annette's ardent admirers. When Keith said he'd like to see Miss Kellerman in person, as he had 'a business proposition to make to her', Jimmie gave him a world-weary look and told him unenthusiastically to run it by him first. Keith, not used to such treatment, left his card and walked away. When Jimmie read it and realised who Keith was, it 'nearly floored him', Annette later claimed.

They tracked Keith down at his Boston hotel. The interview was short and sweet. Keith asked Annette if she thought she could put the whole act on stage. She had absolutely no idea but, determined not to let the opportunity slip, told him blithely 'I don't see why not'. The contract was signed and Jimmie was left to work out the logistics of getting a tank full of water on to a theatre stage. Annette packed her bags and was once again on the move. She was discovering a penchant for travel that would stay with her for the rest of her life. At the height of vaudeville's popularity, she was going to its capital—the bright lights of Broadway were about to shine on the Perfect Woman for all of New York to see.

6

THE BIG TIME: VAUDEVILLE AND NEW YORK CITY

O girl our eyes take in each mystic line,
Your splashes are sweet music, soft, divine,
Your form is like a glint of light
O girl of curves that leads the cultured eye,
 Whence comes that soft caressing breathless sigh
 We utter all and yours by right.

                    (*New York Star*, 7 August 1909, poem by RBH)

When Annette first arrived in New York en route to the White City Amusement Park, she had imagined the city appearing exactly as she had seen it in sketches by the artist Charles Dana Gibson—streets filled with his glamourous Gibson Girls and the Brooklyn Bridge being a mixture of the Champs Élysées and the Pont Neuf. She had been sadly disappointed by the average faces of the New Yorkers and the dull, functional symmetry of the famous bridge. On her return a year later, she hardly had time to notice the city at all. She was whipped straight up on to one of the biggest stages in the New York vaudeville circuit and would quickly surpass the Gibson Girls in both popularity and the American ideal of feminine perfection. She played New York for the next two years.

She made her debut at Keith and Proctor's Fifth Avenue Theatre on 25 November 1908 and was an instant hit. The *New York Star* reported a month later that:

> There's a new Venus in town. She rises from the sea every afternoon and evening at Keith and Proctors. She's a tall handsome Venus, dark of hair, lithe of movement and half sister of Diana. Miss Annette Kellerman is her name. She's as graceful as a mermaid and as daring and as wet when she comes out of the tank after each headlong or footlong dive.

Annette was the headline attraction for seven consecutive weeks and, according to *The Actor's Birthday Book* of 1909, it was 'the record for an act of so heavy a nature'. This referred not to Annette's physique, but to the huge glass tank which Jimmie had somehow managed to manoeuvre on to the stage. It was reputed to hold 25 000 gallons of water.

As far as Annette was concerned, to come straight to vaudeville and headline was to come straight to Heaven and be ushered through the pearly gates without any ifs or buts or beg your pardons. Annette headed a program of tremendous variety— comedy, operetta, dance, animal acts, all vying for the top billing. Vaudeville had something for everyone. At least, this was how it was sold to the American public—as good clean wholesome family entertainment. It was important that vaudeville was perceived to be pure to distinguish it from the other theatrical forms which had spawned it—variety and burlesque. These were marketed towards a working-class audience and were seen as crude and unfit for middle-class families, especially wives and children. It was Keith and Albee who decided to gentrify variety and call it vaudeville—a term which came from a valley, the Vau de Vire, in the French province of Normandy, where the inhabitants were renowned for entertaining one another with ballads and satirical folk songs. As these performers began to entertain outside their valley, their fame spread and over the years the name became corrupted to 'vaudeville'.

With their new name, Albee and Keith built big new theatres across the country and invented their own form of self-censorship. 'The old variety houses used to be filthy places but we changed all that. We believed in soap and water and a strict censorship on stage,' Albee said. Performers were not allowed to say 'slob' or 'son of a gun' or 'Holy Gee' on stage. A notice was posted in the dressing-room of all Keith's theatres: 'If you are guilty of uttering anything sacrilegious or even suggestive you will immediately be closed and will never again be allowed in a theatre where Mr Keith is authority.'

Keith and Albee wanted to lure the middle class to their theatres, so they promoted the idea that it was a safe environment for women. They saw huge profits in soothing the anxieties of moral reformers and, through them, attracting families. Most of the burlesque and variety audiences had been men—and raucous men at that. In Keith's theatres there were signs that asked every gentlemen to please not stamp their feet and wolf whistle 'as it will disturb the ladies'.

The reality of their policy of good clean entertainment was a little different, however. The best-paid acts were women, and they were paid well because they were scantily clad. There were comics whose material was filled with double entendre and singers whose lyrics were amazingly suggestive. Mae West, who came to the stage seven years after Annette, made her career in vaudeville in a show unambiguously called 'Sex'. Her films, tour de forces in the art of double entendre, suggestive lyrics and clothing, were highly censored versions of that show.

Annette fitted perfectly into Keith and Albee's scheme of things: not only was her bathing suit tight-fitting and revealing, but there was the added drawcard of her being wet for most of the show. Annette was one of the few vaudevillians who never drank or smoked or went out to nightclubs after the show. Her grace and skill, and her wholesome attitude to health and life, convinced the public her performances were somehow more tasteful than those of other female entertainers. According to the *Pittsburgh Telegraph*:

> It is something quite apart, not only from any other aquatic specialty but entirely different from any act of any sort that vaudeville has ever given. It is a distinct novelty of the highest class. Miss Kellerman is a beautiful girl with a figure moulded in classic lines and with the contour of a Grecian goddess . . . Every dive is a poem of grace . . . No pure mind would take offence at either the costume or the deportment of *The Diving Venus*. A clever contrivance of mirrors reflects the tank which is sunken to the level of the stage, so that the entire audience may behold the swimmer and diver in every instant of her performance.

Keith and Albee knew exactly what they were doing when they installed the mirrors around the tank in Annette's show. 'Don't you know,' Albee demanded of one of his house managers, 'that what we're selling here is backsides, and that a hundred backsides are better than one.'

The sight of so many backsides was not to everyone's taste. The mayor of East Liverpool NY, His Honour A.V. Schriber, who was well known for championing novel reform measures, was horrified when he saw a 'large and alluring picture of the Diving Venus in flesh coloured tights' advertising Annette's latest performance. He peremptorily had it removed by a policeman. 'I will not tolerate such a thing as that under any circumstances. It is beyond all the bounds of decency. It can't help having a demoralising effect on our young boys,' the Mayor told reporters.

Whether Annette was conscious of the rationale behind Albee's stage design is doubtful. She was confident in her ability to please an audience with what she believed was a tasteful and artistic show, and believed it was her daring dives that drew audiences as much as her one-piece bathing suit. Her act was considered so daring that when she wanted to take out life insurance she was refused. The insurance company reportedly said that 'with Miss Kellerman's diving from such a height into such a very small tank she was likely at any time to either meet with serious accident or kill herself outright'.

Another reason why she may not have suspected her employers' ulterior motives was that she was not some meek little showgirl who would do what ever she was told—she was strong-minded and spoke out directly to the audience if she didn't agree with the circumstances of her performance. For instance, when someone in government suddenly decided that diving was forbidden on Sundays, Annette declared to her audience: 'Ladies and Gentlemen I am sorry that I cannot dive this afternoon. I am as disappointed as you are for I know you don't care a rap for diabolo. There are two husky policemen just outside and there will be a dungeon for me if I dive.'

Though she could be outspoken, Annette did conform in many ways to the unwritten laws for a vaudeville girl. Like most, if not all, female performers, she wore less rather than more and what she did wear diminished as the show went on. Annette would make her first entrance in a long skirt and then whipped that off, revealing a flimsy scarf tied over her tight-fitting one-piece bathing suit. In this outfit she would perform a toe dance and then a 'diabolo' display. This was a popular game at the time, also known as 'the devil on two sticks', which her brother Maurice had taught her on a brief visit to the family in Paris. She would make a double-headed spinning top flip through the air by means of a string attached to two sticks held in each hand. She would then climb up on to a 12 foot springboard from which she would dive into the water and emerge with nothing on but her wet swimming suit. In Annette's case, there was at least a plausible justification for removing her clothes—to swim. For some other performers there was simply no reason at all except that was what the audience expected of a night of good clean family entertainment. Aggie the lion tamer would tame a lion while disrobing and the acrobat Mademoiselle Charmian would remove various articles of clothing after each new acrobatic trick. There was another underwater act by a woman called Odiva, who did not remove clothing, but would remove the skin from a banana and eat it underwater. None of these acts stood the test of time.

Annette was never going to be just another freak act like Mademoiselle Charmian, who only lasted six months, or Peaches Browning, the sixteen-year-old whose famous affair with a millionaire made her notorious enough for a brief career on the vaudeville stage. Notoriety was centrally the initial reason for Keith's interest in Annette. He saw big box office potential in a show in which the star had been both arrested for indecent exposure and declared the Perfect Woman. That she could swim and dive as well was just the icing on the cake. Annette proved she was no flash in the pan by remaining in vaudeville and travelling through America and Europe, entertaining audiences for the next twenty years. *Variety* magazine described her approach:

> Miss Kellerman has won a unique distinction. There is nothing shriekingly loud about her act. She does not resort to the banalities of the abnormal nor to the sickening antics of the wanton in order to attract attention. Candid though she is in the display of the physical beauty nature has so bounteously bestowed on her, there is nothing from her dainty and utilitarian black bathing suit to her most dangerous dive, that would bring a breath of remonstrance from the most straight laced. All is charm and grace and natural adaptability to the exciting and not unnerving things she does. She might well serve as a warning to Charmian, for example, that it is not necessary to be loud in order to be heard, nor unconventional, to use a very pleasant term, in order to make an audience watch every twist of a supple body and turn of a beautifully poised head.

Vaudeville was the first form of mass entertainment—mass corporate-controlled entertainment in the way it is experienced today. The great impresarios were rapidly accumulating theatres across the nation. Acts were booked centrally and routes were planned across the country, making performers national stars. Travelling all year round, performers would play a different theatre every week. An audience in Omaha, Nebraska, would enjoy an act one week in February 1912 and not see it again until March 1913, by which time they would have forgotten their evening's entertainment and it would be new to them again. The difference for Annette was that she was so popular that her first two years in vaudeville were spent almost entirely in

New York. One newspaper reported her at this time as 'one of the biggest stage attractions in the world'.

It is amazing to think that the act which made her so famous lasted only ten minutes in a night that included up to twelve other acts. A typical vaudeville bill would have a 'dumb' show for an opener and usually a 'flash' act for a closer. The number two act would be a 'polite turn'—by which time the audience would have been seated. It was considered chic to walk in late, halfway through the first act, which is why the opening acts were always 'dumb'—animals or pantomimes. It was also the done thing to walk out on the last act. So the top spot, the headline act, always came second last.

When Annette headlined at the Grand Theatre in Pittsburgh in September 1909, her act consisted of a mirror dance and a demonstration of 'diabolo'. She would finish up with a swimming and diving exhibition in the glass tank. Leaping alternately from opposite springboards into a specially prepared tank, she would do a series of dives including; the Neck Dive, where she would balance on the back of her neck, hands on the edge of the board and flip over to enter the water feet first; and the Standing Sitting Dive, where she would stand at the edge of the board, drop down on to her behind and then roll forward and enter the water feet first. She also made front and back dives, but her favourite was 'the Australian Splosh'. Jumping off the board and tucking her knees into her chest, she would enter the water bottom first. The dives were simple compared to today but, because of her ballet training, Annette was graceful and when she first started in vaudeville most people had never seen a diving board, let alone a diver. 'Turning over while in the air and striking the water with either head or feet first is an art which she has mastered in all of its intricacies,' wrote the *Louisville Times* of 1909.

On the bill that night in Pittsburgh, she was followed by actors Claude and Fanny Asher performing a play; the Heim Children then presented a series of songs and dances; a girl called Olive Greatrex showed an astonishing facility to whistle; Mr and Mrs Jimmie Barrie gave a satire; Annie Abbot, the original Georgia Magnet, mystified everybody with her magnetic charms; and Paulinetti and Piquo, European eccentric acrobats, accomplished some fine physical feats.

These were the people who, like Annette, had made it out of the amusement parks and into the big-time vaudeville circuit. And they were good—they had to be. In the face of the latest vaudeville craze an act had always to be prepared to add an extra something. There was no room for stagnation. Acts toured the country and perfected their performances in numerous towns across the 46 (at that time) states of America. Families would grow up never knowing anything but vaudeville and the people on the circuit. The Marx Brothers were one such family. It was a competitive and cut-throat circuit—if an act wasn't brushed up or revamped to keep it snappy, a salary could be cut in half or even quartered.

In those first two years in New York Annette had never been happier. Photographs of her at this time show a slimmer, more streamlined Perfect Woman, dressed in beautiful flowing Edwardian gowns. As was the style of the day, she mostly looked melancholy or pensive with a sorrowful twist to her beautiful neck, but occasionally she was captured with a mischievous dimpled grin which gave a glimpse of the real Annette. She would definitely have been a challenge to the photographer— full of boundless energy, she was seldom still for long enough to be caught on film at all.

'She is moving every minute but doesn't give you the impression of being nervous, but just that she's so full of life that she can't keep still,' is how a reporter from the *Chicago Tribune* described her in December 1910. While performing every night of the week and weekend matinees, Annette still found time to practise fencing, archery and dancing. Her fencing master, Professor Ricardo E. Manriqu, travelled in her retinue when she went on the road, and every day after the matinee, they engaged in lively combat with the swords. If she couldn't play sport, Annette liked to watch it, preferring American football to Rugby, and enjoying baseball and horseracing. She had also just discovered the pleasure of 'autoing'. Automobiles were perfect for Annette's restless temperament—even when she was sitting still, she could be moving. When she advertised for a chauffeur, it made the news pages of the *New York Telegraph*.

> Miss Kellerman wants a chauffeur and a live one. He must have sufficient disrespect for speed laws to be willing to go some. She likes to arrive in a hurry that's why she likes a driver who will open up on a stretch of good road. 'I like to go some myself,' declared the young woman at Hammerstein's Victoria yesterday.

'Annette gets him! She picks out a chauffeur who can make a car whizz for biz' was the headline in the *New York Telegraph* the next day. Twenty-four chauffeurs had arrived to apply for the position and a policeman had to be called in to deal with them when they were told it was taken. The new chauffeur didn't last long. Annette was a terrible back-seat driver and, as soon as she legally could, she began to drive herself. From then on, whenever she had an hour or two free from the theatre, she'd dash out to her car and drive off in any direction, finding relaxation in the fresh air.

One of her first cars was a milk-white monogrammed Buick which she'd thrash up hills that taxed the car to its limit and then turn to her passengers and say 'Look at that!' What she really wanted was to race cars but her mother, hearing about her exploits, had made Annette promise not to race in any big events. However, when she was on tour in Cleveland, she couldn't resist an invitation to race and 'drove the 50 horsepower Buick 63 miles per hour and thereby won to the delight of about 5000 spectators,' reported the *Atlanta Georgian* in March 1911.

Annette loved speed. And, as she told an interviewer much later, at this time in her life she can't remember ever feeling fear. Driving fast came naturally and she did it as often as she could. The *New York Telegraph* reported: 'A big touring car approached, going at a terrific speed. The occupants were a man and a woman. [Policeman] Culbertson chased the machine . . . and commanded the chauffeur to halt. The machine came to a stop. The occupants were Miss Kellerman and her manager Mr Sullivan.'

Annette, who was on her way to perform a matinee, pleaded with them 'piteously' to let her go. It was hard for Culbertson to refuse such a pretty driver but he managed it and took her down to Flatbush station where she was arrested for speeding. She was granted $100 bail—a huge amount of money in those days, but a sum which she was able to produce from her stocking while Culbertson and his superior looked the other way.

This was not her first or her last speeding fine. She became well known to all the police in every town she played. In San Francisco, she was arrested for speeding by the 'only man on the force she wasn't acquainted with'. The judge—whom she also wasn't acquainted with—had, however, seen Annette perform.

When she 'glided into police Judge Conlan's dusky courtroom the sun burst through the fog and a bailiff swore he could hear birds singing'. The judge was visibly perturbed when he saw a vision 'in ethereal blue' take the stand. 'Don't lean on the rim of the desk,' warned the magistrate. 'Other prisoners have leaned there.' This time, although the policeman swore she was speeding, the judge let her off with a warning. For Annette, it was, like her arrest at Boston, all very good publicity.

She was serious about driving, and found it had some very positive health benefits. Though she would never have called herself a feminist—she always described herself as an individualist—Annette could see that men, not women, were enjoying life most. She liked to do the things that men did— drive, swim, fence and ride. Often she was as good, if not better, than them. She wanted other women to share her enjoyment and made it her life's work to convert her sisters to the joys of physical exercise. There was a kind of religiosity in her zeal, but there was also a genuine wish for everyone to feel as good as she did. She advocated swimming as a great sport for women because she loved it and her rickets had been cured by it. She drove because she enjoyed it and wanted others to do so too. She wasn't so much advocating feminism as a more equal distribution of *joie de vivre*.

> There is no pleasure in life greater than running your own machine. This keeps you in the open air, keeps your brain alert, your eye keen, in fact stimulates every one of your senses. It will be a great day for women when the price of an auto is within the reach of everyone.

Women liked Annette. She was often given the equivalent of today's 'up close and personal' interviews by women journalists not always prepared to find her sympathetic. She always won them over. She had a good sense of humour, with no pretensions to great beauty. Mae Tinnee of the *Chicago Tribune* met Annette in 1910:

> She jumped up as quick as a shot . . . and shook hands with me and seemed as glad to see me as if I'd been her long lost sister . . . I reckon I'd better tell you she looks as good as her pictures. In other words she has 'some' figure, as a certain languid young man in our office says. I think her figure's the loveliest thing I've seen since Heck was a pup. Straight and tall and perfectly rounded. She's no Maxine Elliot [a popular stage actress and beauty of the day] when it comes to her face, but it's the kind of face you like. And she has a wide mouth and white teeth and curves in her cheeks when she smiles.

Annette seems to have preferred being photographed from the left profile. The rare frontal shots often show an uneven visage—beautiful, deep-set, grey-green eyes set slightly too close together, a rather too-wide mouth and a strong, square, mannish jaw—but not always. Despite the preponderance of shots taken around this time, she appears different in almost every one. Sometimes she is pretty and sweet and innocent, with dimples and ringlets, and at others she looks stern and uncompromising.

Her self-described 'homely' looks do not seem to have deterred her numerous male admirers. In her first two years in New York, she was besieged by suitors and bemused by the tactics they used to attract her attention. One man, on discovering she spoke French, wrote her a letter in that language begging for a rendezvous and telling her to look out for 'a panama with a red band'. She couldn't believe the silly things these desperate fans wrote to her and their unrequited desires met with no sympathy, as she told the *Pittsburgh Leader*:

> 'Chere petite', dear little one—that's me—dear little one—and I'm not little, whatever I am and I'm not his dear or anyone else's either. He thinks I'm adorable, isn't that sweet of him? He wouldn't think so if he knew how much I was laughing at him. Kind of mean too, but he ought to know better.

Nor would Annette tolerate bad behaviour from men in the audience when she was on stage. When she was about to make a second dive into the tank at one performance, a young man in the front row shouted, 'Gee, you're a peach!'. Annette turned and glared at the man, walked to the end of the diving board, then 'jumped in the direction of the front row and aimed to flood'. She pulled her knees up to her chest and threw herself in with all her weight. It was a fine example of the Australian Splosh and she struck the offender right in the face. As he left rather shamefacedly, Annette was heard to remark 'and I think that should teach him better manners'. She had also unfortunately totally doused the orchestra leader, Professor Ward Johnson, who took it in his stride, shook the water from his baton and counted the orchestra back in.

Beneath her bravado Annette was genuinely disturbed by the behaviour of her male fans. What she really wanted was to meet 'nice men' who weren't underhand, didn't use false names or propose secret rendezvous. 'I like to please people,' she said in an interview with the *Indianapolis Star*. 'I like to give them their money's worth and do all I can to make my act a success. But outside of that I want to enjoy my life like any other girl. And

I will too. I'm only twenty-two: and I don't want to fall in love yet—for if I do, I'll be awfully in love.'

However, 'other girls' were neither the Perfect Woman nor the most popular act in town. Though Jimmie had negotiated a good deal for Annette at Wonderland and what seemed to be favourable terms with B.F. Keith, neither of them imagined quite the impact she would make in New York. Opening on Broadway in late 1908, by April 1909 she was the Queen of the Auto Carnival, receiving 40 000 votes from fans—four times as many as her rivals. It was the first modern automobile parade down Fifth Avenue, and all the car companies had different floats. Buick built a huge sea shell with mermaids and a throne for their Queen. The day was not exactly balmy, and Annette, in a fishtail and not much else, says in 'My Story' that she felt more like a snow queen as she waved to muffled, fur-coated spectators. Finally she arrived at the Majestic Theatre where a special performance of *Cavilliera Rusticana* and *I Pagliaci* was staged for her benefit.

It was a heady time. Annette was only twenty-two and Jimmie, her manager, just a year older. When they were offered a contract by William Morris to perform in his theatres for $1500 a week—five times the amount that Keith was paying— they signed up without hesitation. Morris contracted her up for the summer season only, and had no objection to her working for Keith in the winter. Annette and Jimmie seemed to have forgotten the fact that she was already under contract to Keith. He hadn't.

The court case began in April and continued for months. Annette and Jimmie were hopelessly out of their depth in dealing with the two entrepreneurs battling for her billing. The Keith circuit was the most powerful in the business, and was to retain

its stranglehold until the early 1930s. But Morris wasn't far
behind. Coming to the country as an immigrant, he became the
world's foremost theatrical agent and was the personal manager
and founder of the Morris agency which still today boasts some
of Hollywood's most famous stars. The rivalry between the
Morris and Keith theatrical empires had a history of feuding—
and now they were engaged in a no-holds barred battle to the
death. The fight for Annette was just one of many between the
two magnates. They had the best lawyers in the country, Keith
having hired the president's attorney and brother, Mr Taft, as
his counsel. The first thing Taft did was to take out an injunction
to stop Annette performing for Morris at all. Taft was reported
to have received a retainer of $2500 while Annette's team of
lawyers—attorney Geo. M. Leventritt, with William Guthrie
and Benjamin P. Cardoza as counsel—received $1000 each.
Things went against Annette from the start. On 10 April 1909,
Judge Ward of the United States Circuit Court decided Annette
was to be restrained from appearing under any other management than Keith's. Annette had been performing at William
Morris's American Theatre but had not been able to give her
full act due to a temporary injunction taken out before the
decision. She was in the extremely uncomfortable position of
being permitted to appear in her one-piece bathing suit but to
do little or nothing else—a high diver called Speedy went through
the act in her place.

   The situation came to a head on the night before Annette
was crowned the Queen of the Auto Carnival when she was
'captured' by Morris's men. After what *Variety* magazine described
as an 'all night confab', she agreed to appear at Morris's American
Theatre. The next day, when the parade had ended, Keith's man
from the legal department, Maurice 'the go and get 'em kid'

Goodman, came round to persuade Annette to fulfil her contract to play that night at the Fifth Avenue Theatre. Jimmie tried to convince her to stick with Morris. Two of Morris's men then appeared on the scene to back up Annette's manager, but 'Annie Kelly stuck to her guns and decided to stay with the Keith colours'. Perhaps she realised that Keith was too powerful to resist, or perhaps she just didn't like being pushed around—especially by Jimmie. Goodman got Annette to the theatre just in time to make her entrance. The planks which covered the tank and kept it warm, were lifted to reveal an empty pool. Someone (almost certainly one of the Morris men) had literally pulled the plug. The tank took 40 minutes to refill and heat. The audience waited while the exhausted Annette, alone in the wings, shivered in her cotton swimsuit. She was used to wearing silk but that suit was, along with all her other costumes, laid out ready for her in the dressing-room of the American Theatre.

Rumours were rife about the salary she would receive from the bidding melee, ranging from $2500–$3000 a week. Journalists weren't impressed with such behaviour, calling her a 'Flopper'— a performer who would do a 'flip flop' (as in the handstand that flips from side to side) from one theatrical manager to the next to receive the best salary. *Variety* expressed the opinion that:

> Miss Kellerman is now our grandest little flopper. She and Mr Sullivan are rapidly becoming known as two people with not a thought in the world worth hanging on to. If the hide-and-go-seek continues Miss Kellerman will likely have a theatre named after her . . . with a guarantee the courts will attend to no other business while she is in New York.

Though the press might not have approved, the publicity of the court case created a feeding frenzy around the Diving Venus.

Everyone wanted a piece of the hottest act in town, and Annette just couldn't refuse. While the case was proceeding in court, she was offered a particularly lucrative sum of money to make some short films featuring her diving skills. They were shown on five or ten cent slot machines. Also known as kinescope machines, these permitted only one viewer at a time. There was a thick black cotton cloth under which the viewer would place their head. Once under they would look into a small, face-sized screen. Rows of these were installed in kinescope parlours and existing entertainment venues such as penny arcades. The short one- or two-reel films were often titillating and voyeuristic, like the method of viewing. Though called *The Art of Diving*, Annette's films were obviously not just made to educate future divers, as the film's publicity points out:

> She is seen to the utmost advantage in the famous black tights upon which the sun glints lovingly . . . the dripping silk of the fleshings appears almost iridescent as the angle of reflection is changed with each sinuous move.

For a moment, Morris and Keith were on the same side— both had her name on a contract and were charging substantially more than five or ten cents for her vaudeville performances.

When they heard about the kinescope deal, they repeatedly 'threatened to do all sorts of legal things to her again'. The press was sarcastic. The *New York Herald* said: 'Naturally the young lady posed with avidity and pocketed the big fat check with great glee.'

Sitting at the Bench of the US Circuit Court, Judge Hough looked down severely on the smartly dressed woman, her manager and their lawyers. He was not impressed by the defence, especially when Annette declared she had signed the Morris contract without knowing its contents. His comments were reported in the *New York Star* of 15 May 1909:

> Consideration of the affidavits in this case, as well as those in the previous litigation, convince me that neither Miss Kellerman nor her manager has the slightest regard for business honour; indeed they seem incapable of understanding the obligations of a contract, and if their affidavits were important in deciding any matter of fact I should hesitate to accept the statements of either without ample corroboration.

Eventually the case was settled, and Annette was enjoined to fulfil her contract to Keith. She was to go back to work for him for only $1250 a week, $250 less than Morris had given her. It was the first time a vaudeville manager had won so complete a victory over such a contract, and the case made it much more difficult for a performer to break a contract with a manager from then on. However, this didn't seem to work the other way. Later, when other Diving Venuses came along, Keith was able to halve Annette's salary while keeping her working just as much.

When she went back to work for Keith in April 1909 it all seemed settled. On 5 May Morris counter-sued Annette for breach of contract. On 9 May, *Variety* reported:

> The betting on Broadway was even money Miss Kellerman would play the week out for Keith, and 2–1 she would 'flop' to Morris before Sunday. 7–5 was laid that if she flopped to Morris by Sunday she would flop back to Keith by Monday. Artists are discussing the case with disgust and it is estimated the disgust will cost the vaudeville managers $85,000 in increased salaries for the next season.

On 11 May Judge Hough ruled that William Morris Inc. had no claim on the services of Annette Kellerman. According to the *New York Telegraph*, he then 'denied the application for an injunction to restrain her from appearing under any other management'. It had been a long and expensive lesson for Annette and Jimmie. From that time on they were far more circumspect when signing agreements. In her memoirs, Annette says little about the case except that it cost Keith $25 000 and, as predicted in *Variety*, he made the theatres pay an extra hundred dollars over and above her wage to allay the added expense. Keith was a powerful man, and he got his money's worth. 'I played for two years without a day's vacation,' Annette wrote in *How to Swim*.

Meanwhile, the show had to go on. Although the summer vaudeville season was over, Annette was still the most popular act in town. Her fans were just as keen as ever and 'the shapely diver taxed the capacity (of the theatre) at every performance'. A year later, Robert Grau, an early commentator, described her as:

The Queen of Modern Vaudeville. Annette Kellerman's appearance in a vaudeville theatre at this time is an event of such importance that at the opening sale of seats in any auditorium where she is announced one would suppose a Bernhardt or a Pattie (the famous soprano) was scheduled to appear.

In the summer of 1909, though she was as popular as ever with her audience, the outcome of the court case was still affecting the way Annette's fellow performers treated her. To 'flop' was considered bad form. One gesture in the heat of a New York summer went a long way to redress the situation. At this time, she was performing at Hammerstein's Roof Garden.

With the proliferation of skyscrapers on the New York skyline at the turn of the century, roof gardens became very popular venues in the summer season. They were also a great deal cooler than street level. The famous Madison Square Roof Garden, built in 1890, was designed by the infamous Stanford White who was shot dead there by an enraged husband in 1906. Hammerstein's Victoria Theatre opened in 1899 and was inspired by White's construction. It originally housed the 'Venetian Terrace Roof Garden', a café and petting zoo, but in 1901 this was converted to a theatre which was re-opened on 26 June as the 'Paradise Roof Garden', more commonly known as Hammerstein's Roof. It was a large space open at either end, closed along the sides, and had delicate wrought-iron pillars holding up a flat roof. A performer standing centre stage would have seen elaborately decorated loges down the left-hand side while on the right were the bleachers in between which were the stalls. The space could seat up to 900 people. Annette recalled in one of her last interviews (quoted in *The Australian* after her death) that Charlie Chaplin was playing Hammerstein's at the same time. 'You know we started off together. He was playing comedy down below and I was upstairs in the roof garden.'

When Annette came to perform, the manager, William Hammerstein (father of Oscar, the famous librettist) had drilled a $3000 hole to install her tank. Not long afterwards, the *New York Sun* reported that she had heard the showgirls next door at the Lyric were struggling through each Wednesday matinee in the heat. She invited them to come and have a swim in the tank. They were so grateful, and had such fun playing around like 'frisky sea lions', that Annette invited them back every Wednesday for the rest of the warm spell.

Annette's act inspired many women to take up swimming in the hope of achieving her perfect proportions. She began to publish a series of articles in the newspaper on how to swim, which became so popular that the *New York Telegraph* reported 'a rush of fat folk to the sea. Yesterday fourteen women, not one of them under two hundred pounds, were spotted splashing in the green sea'. It was the start of a parallel career. Beginning with newspaper articles, she then went on to lecture women on the benefits of exercise in every town she played. One of the earliest women attempting a scientific study of fitness, Annette was now pioneering a path for the showbusiness fitness gurus of the future.

7
PHYSICAL BEAUTY AND HOW TO KEEP IT

Annette stood at the lectern in a tight-fitting black velvet gown before hundreds of women. She was a little nervous. Not in her wildest dreams had she imagined that her talks would be so well attended. It was a morning matinee, and hundreds of women had already been turned away. Her eyes scanned the audience— there was not a man in the house, only women of all different shapes and sizes, and all of them looking to her to disclose the secret to becoming the Perfect Woman. They were wearing the beautifully moulded gowns of the turn of the century, tight-fitting around the chest and waist, then flowing in layers to the floor. Beautiful but awkward. To achieve the desired shape, corsets and pins and tucks were needed underneath to support the structure. The gowns and corsets made walking difficult and hid a variety of defects. Annette found it tremendously irritating that women were constantly hampered by the demands of fashion. She would later design comfortable and simple clothing which sold all over the world. She had a steadfast belief that creating more ergonomic fashions and designs was more immediately liberating than any political movement of the time. It took a certain type of woman to throw herself in front of a horse to achieve universal suffrage. Most women, though they wanted change, could feel they were at least doing something towards improving their circumstances by changing the way they dressed.

Annette told her audience that a girl is constantly reminded of what she can't do. Getting older meant the restrictions would become more limiting. As she wrote in *How to Swim*, a woman is corseted and gowned and 'thoroughly imbued with the idea that it is most unladylike to be possessed of legs or to know what to do with them . . . and yet she manages fairly well as a land animal and accommodates her steps to hampering petticoats with a fair degree of skill'.

The audience tittered uncomfortably, but Annette was not letting them off the hook lightly. One thing the Diving Venus knew how to do well was to speak her mind. She was reported in the *New York Evening Journal* of 11 May 1912 as saying:

> Wear your new hobble skirt and tight waist, your hat which comes over your eyes like blinders and go into a crowded section of the city and try to cross the street, you will just naturally wait for the policeman to pilot you over because your clothes will make you timid. The corset has done more to make physical cowards of women than any other thing since slavery. You cannot be brave if your diaphragm is squeezed and you can't breathe properly.

It was radical talk in 1912, when a middle-class woman wouldn't leave the house without first having her maid lace her into her stays of whalebone and elastic, crushing her ribs and then holding a bottle of smelling salts to her nose when she fainted. Corsets were one of Annette's *bêtes noirs*. They were, she said in *Physical Beauty: How to Keep It*, 'fiendish things injurious both to body and health', caused 'endless harm and misery in the world' and, when tightly laced, 'were nothing short of an artificial deformity'.

After the lecture the women in the audience stormed the stage demanding: 'Do you wear a rubber corset under your bathing suit?' She explained that they could make their own 'muscular' corset through proper diet and exercise and proceeded to use her own body as an example. The breathless fashion editor at the *New York Telegraph* reported her scandalous actions in an article with the headline 'Diving girl shows how shape is all nature made':

> The swimming Venus looked as if the most expert of couturiers had moulded her into creation. She proved in startling fashion that this wasn't so. 'I'll just rip this thing (her black gown) off,' said the confidential Annette, suiting the action to the word and revealing herself in her black swimming suit. Then I'll just rip this thing (the bathing suit) down the side and show you that there's nothing underneath but—but me,' and she did that too.

The lecture thrilled the audience, who managed to gasp copiously—despite their corsets. Annette believed that, from then on, American women became figure conscious. That first lecture was a strange mixture of showbiz razzamatazz and a revival meeting. Before the ripping of the swimsuit, Annette performed a display of fencing with Professor Ricardo E. Manriqu, her fencing master, who then was supposed to quickly disappear. However, he was spotted later by an observant reporter as he was peeping in the wings and was ready to ratify everything Miss Kellerman said. He later told the *Pittsburgh Leader*, 'she does not wear the thing described by crass, uncultivated minds as "the corset"'.

Annette lectured to capacity houses of women in every city she toured. Her popularity was so great that she had to establish an office in Broadway. She self-published her first book, *The Body Beautiful*, to deal with an overwhelming stream of inquiries. It was sold by mail order. Her ad boasted: 'If you are too thin, too fleshy, undeveloped or unshapely, if your complexion is sallow, if you are weak, ill, tired or languid, or in any respect not as nature meant you to be, send for my booklet.'

Unfortunately now lost, it was, according to one smitten writer in *Mumsey's* magazine, 'the most interesting and attractive book' he'd ever read. Annette received and answered between 100 and 200 letters a day from women wanting to know how to obtain a good figure, a healthy body and a healthy mind, and she was personally teaching 75 New York society women how to swim and dive. Such was her success in New York that there were plans afoot to build an 800-room health resort for women on a 350 acre property in Pennsylvania. She was also negotiating to buy one of the best hotels and beaches on Coney Island. Neither of these plans seems to have come to fruition.

In terms of what women should wear and eat and achieve with their lives, Annette was way ahead of her time in most of the ideas she put forward, and she challenged women to think differently about themselves. Eventually these ideas were more formally synthesised into *Physical Beauty: How to Keep It*. It was a refreshingly straightforward book that covered every facet of how to be beautiful—from diets and clothing to facial hair and pimples.

As with everything she did, her newspaper articles and later books were thoroughly researched. In contrast to other authors of the day, she was scientific rather then dreamy-eyed about beauty. Mrs Roger Watts (whose book *The Renaissance of the Greek Ideal* was recommended on the back page of *Physical Beauty*) based her ideas of attaining physical perfection on her 'careful study of Greek statuary and vases and by research in literature'.

Annette's books were far more modern. With the help of simple exercises a woman could do at home, she gave practical advice on how to improve the female form. Her methods were sometimes confronting. She advised her readers to stand in front of the mirror naked and examine themselves. If they were honest about it they'd be able to see pretty clearly what the problem was. If not, she could help them a little further. 'Is your flesh firm or is it loose or wobbly? Now bend over in various attitudes. Are there unsightly wrinkles and rolls of loose flesh?' And just to make sure they knew exactly what loose flesh was, she advised readers to lie on their backs, then strain forward as if about to sit up and hold the position while grabbing their abdomens:

> If you are thin there will be rolls of skin no bigger than your fingers, if you are moderate there should be a half inch or so depth of fatty tissue as large as a broom handle. But if you are too fat there will be big rolls of loose flesh above the tightened muscles.

It's not difficult to imagine Annette examining her own body in just such detail. She was never dishonest about her own defects, always being the first to point them out with disparaging humour as she said to the *Pittsburgh Leader*:

> When I say exercise and diet will make a woman healthy and beautiful I don't mean she'll have a classical nose and gorgeous blonde hair. I have about three hairs myself and I don't approve

of my nose at all. I mean a woman can acquire vitality, health, magnetism and symmetry.

Annette expected her readers to be as blunt and truthful with themselves as she was with herself. However, they were not to feel sorry for themselves—she never did. Instead she came up with positive ways to make the best of a bad situation. Throughout her life and all the ups and downs of her career, she never felt self-pity or regret. When her vaudeville career began to wind down Annette created her own shows, and when demand for those diminished she would work on charity projects to keep busy. She exercised daily almost until the day she died.

'I always advocate something to do for every woman as a first step to keeping young,' she wrote in the *New York Evening Journal*. 'Stagnation always means age, when it doesn't mean death.'

Annette had the physical fitness of an athlete, and her fame was comparable to the big Hollywood movie stars of today, but she had achieved all this without cosmetic surgery, Pilates or personal trainers. To the average housewife of the time, Annette appeared so physically perfect as to be almost another gender. Fans crowded to get a glimpse of her or to touch her.

Almost immediately, the physical fitness lectures made money and there were other spin-off businesses that were flourishing as well, including Kellerman hats and bathing suits designed by Annette. On 5 December 1909, the *New York Telegraph* predicted:

[She] may at no distant day be the richest woman on stage. One business alone took $7000 last week and her bank account is assuming proportions when, should one investment go wrong, the loss of such a sum as $50 000 would be considered only an incident.

It was Frederick Kellerman's rather Victorian philosophy of 'duty' that was always the guiding principle behind his daughter's career. It must never be simply showbiz for showbiz's sake; there had to be a good moral foundation supporting everything one did. Frederick believed that Annette, like her mother, was not just a performer. Alice had made a great difference to the appreciation and growth of music and musical society in Sydney at the end of the nineteenth century, and was awarded by the French government for her achievements. Frederick often told Annette that she too had something to give back to the society she was living in, and could, by her example, show what a healthy life could do for the young girls and women of America. Naturally Annette was drawn to studying the scientific and moral aspects of physical fitness at an early age. From the time of her Broadway debut at twenty-two, she was writing articles with a surprisingly authoritative air. She knew what she was talking about, and felt it was her duty to enlighten the rest of society.

Though Annette may have appeared to her legions of fans like a star from another solar system, she certainly didn't play the part. She was popular because she never spoke down to her public—their problems were her problems, and she dealt with them humourously. Her talks always began with the phrase: 'It's going to be an awfully informal lecture.' She would tackle any problems, big or small, with a breezy confidence and her attention to detail always came up with practical solutions.

Annette also analysed the discrepancies between what marriage meant for a man and what it meant for a woman. Women, she said in *Physical Beauty*, were bred to be at the height of their beauty in order to attract a suitable husband, but once they were married they had no right to remain beautiful.

Love, we are told, is an incident to a man but the great fundamental fact of a woman's existence. But should a woman once married try to keep her body beautiful she is accused of seeking further loves . . . All our religion and morality has failed to keep men good—if by goodness we mean for a man to remain faithful in spirit, as well as in the flesh, to the love of a woman who loses her physical attractiveness.

As Annette saw it, the truth of divorce and marital unhappiness was basically that a wife lost her charm for her husband. 'The average woman takes it as a matter of course that she shall "settle down" after marriage,' she wrote in the *Syracuse Post Standard*. 'And she usually settles down with a thump.' Her image of married life after the 'thump', when women would stop trying and let go, is almost Dante-esque:

As a result we have hundreds of shapeless young and middle-aged women—fat, shapeless, loose, engaged in a continuous struggle with their buttons; or scrawny umbrellas of women, with every curve a hollow and every bone trying to make itself felt and seen.

While she wasn't advocating anything as revolutionary as a wife leaving her husband, Annette was addressing the problem in a radical way. Instead of recommending powders, miracle potions and corsets to stay young and beautiful, she was giving women the opportunity to do it themselves—through exercise. In one way it was a simplistic solution to a myriad of complex marital problems. However, she had also come up with a simple program for making women feel better—not just a series of exercises, but a whole new way of living. She had exercises for everything from improving your breasts to strengthening the lower limbs; advice about diet and skin care; instruction on how to dance and breathing exercises. Long before yoga had become popular in the Western world, she knew about the yogic breathing practised by what she described as the 'picturesque priests of the Orient'. Her descriptions of deep-breathing and relaxation techniques are obviously derived from a knowledge of yoga and are remarkably simple and modern.

In *Physical Beauty* Annette makes a compelling argument for women who were stuck at home with the daily drudge of children, washing and housework. There was another way to live:

> If only you could realise what it is to waken in the morning feeling that the day is not possibly long enough to let you live as much as you wanted to, if only you could know what it is to walk and work and play and feel every inch of you rejoicing in glorious buoyant life, there is not one of you who would not say, 'Teach me! Teach me!'

Like Isadora Duncan, she also encouraged women to dance:

> Put on a record. Listen to it. What does it make you feel? What does it make you think? Play it again and dance your thought. Don't be self conscious. Don't pay any attention to the long faced moralist who tells you dancing is only 'hugging set to music'. Don't listen to him or teach *him* to dance.

As she made clear in her lectures, she also wanted women to throw off the shackles of burdensome clothing: 'As soon as you are physically uncomfortable you are under a strain, and no-one can do good work or be really happy if physical discomfort is allowed to continue.' She appealed to women's commonsense, in her *New York Evening Journal* article: 'Don't you think it's very unintelligent to be uncomfortable and give up your freedom merely to ape foolish fashions set by the men dressmakers who laugh at us for wearing them?'

When it came to fashion Annette believed that comfort was more important than convention. In 1916 she designed her 'shirt dresses': wool jersey, long-sleeved shirts extended to the ankle to become a dress, flexible and comfortable and prominently not featuring a corset underneath. They were a forerunner to the simple bold designs of the 1920s, and were copied all over the world. But, especially when she was young, Annette enjoyed showing off the most perfect form in the world with fashions that were original and fun, though not always functional. As the *New York Telegraph* stated:

> Some of Miss Kellerman's clothes, all of which are entirely her own ideas and original in conception, are almost barbaric in their conception and Spanish in their design. One gown of which she is particularly fond is a princess messaline blue shot with red. The bodice to this is made of thread gold, fitting snugly with elbow sleeves. Draped over this are two beautiful crepe de chene [*sic*] shawls of paisley design with wide red boarders, the only two in this country.

When she couldn't find a hat she wanted, she created some very original designs. After buying a white fur coat to go with her new white Buick, Annette wanted a hat to match, but there weren't any—so she bought a fur muff and put in on her head, telling the surprised sales girl: 'This will do splendidly, thank you.' Annette looked the absolute height of fashion when reporters snapped her at the wheel of her Buick convertible in a white fur coat and matching hat. It was actually a joke in theatrical circles, and particularly with close friends, that Annette never bought hats: 'She will wear a lampshade from her hotel room and make it becoming if nothing else chances near,' reported the *Atlanta Georgian*.

It was her revolutionary one-piece bathing suit, however, that really made the most lasting impact on American society at the beginning of the twentieth century. By the time she came to write *Physical Beauty and How to Swim* in 1918, the frilly corseted bathing suits of ten years earlier were beginning to disappear and many women had taken to wearing Annette's simple design: a body-hugging swimsuit covered with a tunic for modesty. Naturally Annette believed swimming to be the best exercise for women. Having cured her childhood rickets, she believed that swimming could work wonders for the rest of womankind. It was a graceful art that suited women better than men. What was more, as she had proved in the Seine and in the English Channel, women could equal, if not surpass, men in the water. At the time, statistics quoted in the *Atlanta Georgian* showed that in long-distance swimming women came within 10 per cent of equalling men. The reasons she gave for this phenomenon are still valid today, that women have more fatty tissue than men and this helps in two ways—fat is lighter than muscle and helps in staying afloat, and over long distances it insulates.

She attributed all sorts of benefits to the art of swimming— not only in beautifying the outer body but in working miracles on the inside. Sluggish kidneys and livers, constipation, unsightly pimples and ugly blotches could all be cured by swimming.

In the same way that self-help authors today give examples of miraculous cures, Annette told the tale of Dorothy Becker, who was on death's door with an unspecified malady. One day the little girl begged her father to teach her to swim in the ocean. Finally her father yielded, little Dorothy learned to swim, and within a month had regained perfect health. She became known as the 'Champion Mermaid of Sacramento'. Probably more convincing for readers today is Annette's simple description of the benefits of an occasional swim, quoted in the *Atlanta Georgian*: 'That weary feeling goes away for once in the cool quiet water. Tired men and women forget that stocks and cakes have fallen.'

For Annette, swimming was something more; it represented survival. When she worked on Broadway, instead of going to bars or nightclubs after the show, she would drive off in a hurry for her 'nightcap' at the beach. A quick dip at the end of the night was her way of dealing with the demands of stardom and of 'keeping her soul modest'. When she had swum far enough from the shore, she described herself as seeming to 'shrink and shrink 'til I was nothing but a flecky bubble and feared that bubble would burst'. To Annette there was nothing more democratic than 'swimming out beyond the surf line . . . Everyone is happy and young and funny. No one argues. No one scolds. There is no time and no place where one may so companionably play the fool and not be called one.' Ironically, even though swimming was her sanity, during their long and happy marriage Annette's husband was always afraid of the water and couldn't swim a stroke.

8
MORE THAN A FRIENDLY INTEREST

Annette stood in the wings at Keith and Proctor's Fifth Avenue theatre in New York, waiting for her diving scene to be set up on stage. Sometimes she still couldn't believe that she was in New York—or that she was one of the most popular stars in vaudeville. She was surrounded by the muffled conversations of fellow performers in other acts waiting in the wings when she heard her name mentioned. She recognised the voices of the two comedians who came on a couple of acts further down the bill. 'Aw, she's just a passing fad. As soon as the novelty wears off she'll be back in the Ten-twenty and thirties.'

'Yeah,' said the other. 'You've got to have much more than a fine shape to make a lasting impression in the US of A.'

Annette had a sinking feeling in the pit of her stomach. She had never considered a life other than theatre; it was all she had ever wanted. But what alternative was there for a woman except marriage? She had had literally hundreds of admirers, but had never even considered giving up her career for any of them. Marriage was something other women did. 'Marry?' she told one interviewer, 'No indeed. I'm too ambitious for that. If only American girls had more pluck and go-ahead spirit they would not be contracting marriage as a necessity which I never intend to do.'

She was not about to give up her career. But perhaps it was her career that was giving up on her? In that case, maybe she would have to consider marriage. But of all the gentlemen who admired her, there wasn't really anyone she knew well enough to even like, let alone fall in love with. Jimmie saw to that; he was very good at keeping the wolves from the door.

There was one gentleman who had sent her a very nice letter. He had been in Australia once and had received splendid treatment, and he was anxious to return the compliment. He wondered whether Annette would accept a little Christmas gift and a box of champagne. He also offered his limousine (a rare beast in those days) and, if she liked cruising, his luxury yacht was at her disposal. The doorman put down the box of champagne and held out a small parcel to Annette. When she opened it, they both gasped. 'Lying in a lovely satin case was a magnificent diamond and emerald bracelet,' she said in 'My Story'. She went straight to her dressing-room and sent for Jimmie. She was surprised that this gift had got past his eagle eye and wanted to show him. She always told him the silly things that her admirers said and did, and they usually had a laugh together. But this one was a little different, and she thought she wouldn't mind meeting him. When she showed Jimmie the jewellery, he didn't laugh at all. It was the first time she'd seen him angry.

'Why the big so and so!' he said to Annette. 'Get the maid to pack them right away and you send that parcel right back. You have to watch out for that kind.'

She would have taken this from no one else but Jimmie. After all, her father had chosen him to look after her when he left for Paris. She sent the bracelet back, but gave the champagne to the stagehands and a merry Christmas was had by all.

Annette had actually contemplated marriage once before, in the early days in America when she was playing White City. A young doctor had come to every show and waited patiently afterwards in the dusty showground lanes outside the concession to have a word with her—in the presence of her father, of course. It was he who had taught her to play golf while Jimmie took Aunt Josephine out to museums. Moving to Boston to play Wonderland was 'the only thing that saved the Wedding Bells', she wrote in 'My Story'. The young doctor, though tall, good looking and perfectly well mannered, was soon forgotten in the excitement of Boston and then New York. It was almost too much excitement sometimes for a twenty-year-old girl, but Annette said in her memoirs that good old Jimmie 'was always there to steady me up'.

The young doctor had not forgotten *her*. How could he? Her name was in every paper. One day he knocked on her dressing-room door saying that he simply couldn't get her out of his mind, Chicago was lonely without her, would she consider making him the happiest man on Earth? Annette, still rankling from the conversation she had heard in the wings earlier, was tempted but not sure. She asked him whether she could take a few days to decide and, when he left, immediately consulted Jimmie. She reported the conversation in 'My Story'.

'Well, it's none of my business, but he'd never last six months with you. You'd want to be up and doing inside of six weeks.'

'How do you happen to know so much about it?' asked Annette.

'Listen, I've known you ever since you came over to this country with your dad. What's more, I know you much better than you know yourself.'

Annette was about to ask him exactly what he meant when he turned and left the room. It was strange, he usually stayed for a chat after the show. Annette decided she would prove him wrong and said 'yes' to the doctor.

'Diving Venus to wed physician' the headlines read. The engagement doesn't seem to have lasted long. Maybe it was the thought of being like all those other American girls 'contracting marriage as a necessity', or perhaps it was the fact that she just couldn't give up showbiz, but what was certain was that Jimmie had been right: she couldn't stay the course. Though it made the headlines, there's no mention anywhere of the engagement or the doctor again in her memoirs.

Annette decided to stay and face her critics, and was determined to be more than just a 'fine shape'. As usual, Jimmie was there to help. Every day for two hours she worked with New York's finest ballet master, Luigi Albertieri of the Metropolitan Opera House. With her new-found confidence, she made dynamic changes to her show. Somehow she even persuaded the pathologically shy Jimmie to appear with her—a feat which reveals the depth of his devotion. The show was now set in Dieppe, a beach in the summer, with a bathhouse stage left. The *New York Telegraph* reported:

The perfect woman approaches the ocean attired in skirts and enters the bathhouse. She is closely followed by her manager Mr Sullivan, who has turned pantomimic actor. He is armed with a camera and he waits to snap the Perfect Woman when she reappears. Miss Kellerman keeps neither him nor the spectators waiting. She trips out minus a skirt but wearing dancing shoes, a tiny waist [a fringed silk scarf] and her tight-fitting one-piece bathing suit. Then she proceeds to do some toe dancing followed by her 'diabolo' display. Having displayed her skill in these lines she dashes up to a springboard twelve feet above the water and plunges in waist and all. She emerges after having in some miraculous way divested herself of the waist. From her shoulders to her feet Annette is covered by the suit which closely clings to the lines of her agile form.

The new show was even more successful than the last. And all thoughts of marriage were banished. There were plenty of reasons for a top-billing female vaudeville star not to marry. One of Annette's contemporaries, Mae West, made the mistake of marrying young, before she became famous. She quickly rectified the matter by divorcing her husband and subsequently became *very* famous. She made sure she never married again. From being a top vaudeville star, she went on to become one of the richest and most powerful women in Hollywood in the 1930s. She was one of the few actors in the rigid studio system who had control of the vehicle she starred in. She wrote and performed in her films, and chose who was to direct and star with her. At that time, most men would not tolerate a wife who had a career and, if they did, the marriage usually ended in divorce or with the husband taking over the management of his wife's career—making a mess of everything. Even as late as the 1940s and 1950s, this was occurring. Esther Williams (who was to initiate and star in the bio pic of Annette's life, *Million Dollar Mermaid*) was making large sums of money in 1950s Hollywood and was horrified to find, when her career started to tail off in the 1960s, that her husband/manager had lost it all on bad investments, gambling and heavy drinking.

Annette, who had been on the verge of giving up everything she loved, became far more cautious with her admirers in the future. By this time everybody knew the manager had fallen for the boss—everybody except the boss. She was busy preparing for a season at the Palace Theatre in London. Since she had last been there, Annette's show was far more sophisticated and created a great stir. She had no time to think about her manager and was totally unaware of how he felt about her. Performing twice a day in the West End, she attracted a whole new swathe of admirers. There was one gentleman who waited outside the stage door after every performance, rain or shine, with flowers and chocolates. One day, totally out of character, Jimmie came to her dressing-room in a towering rage. When Annette asked him what was the matter, he burst into an angry tirade, which she wrote about in 'My Story'.

> Listen, I've played nursemaid to you ever since I came to work for your father. Up to now things have gone fairly well. But that 'tramp' who's been hanging around the stage door is just another 'Stage Door John'. He's no good and I'm telling him so, pronto!

No one, especially nice, sweet, kind, reliable Jimmie, had ever talked to Annette in this way. She didn't like it at all.

'Well, you've got a lot of cheek but if you want to know something he doesn't mean a thing to me,' she said, and then she added with her sweetest smile, 'His chocolates and flowers are nice though.'

It was the straw that broke the poor lovesick manager's back. Annette later wrote:

Jimmie came up to me, took me by the arms and shook me and banged my head against the wall. I was mad too, but imagine my surprise when he took me in his arms and said, 'Oh Sweet, I'm sorry.' Then he rushed from the room leaving me gasping. You could have knocked me down with a feather but after that incident I began to look at 'Mr Jimmie' with new 'Lenses'.

It was while she was spending a weekend at a stately English home that Annette began to realise how 'really grand' Jimmie was. She remembered all the kind sweet things he'd done for her. Looking back, she began to realise that it was not long after her father's death that Jimmie had begun to take more than a friendly interest in her. While the guests at the house party were wonderful to her, and she was flattered by the attentions of the smitten son of the house, the experience only made her miss Jimmie more. All she could think about was getting back to the Palace Theatre as soon as possible.

When at last she was sitting in the dressing-room after a show and Jimmie finally came in, all he could manage to ask, rather sheepishly, was whether she had had a good time. She was awfully tongue-tied too, but said awkwardly: 'Yes, but I missed you.' Jimmie blurted out: 'Gee, did you?' They stood there smiling inanely at each other for a little longer and then both suddenly had to leave. From that moment on they were constantly running away from each other. Later Jimmie told Annette that at this time he was afraid he wasn't the right person for her. He was sure she would marry someone rich. Meanwhile, Annette was avoiding Jimmie as much as possible. For the first time her feelings for him were stronger than she'd ever felt for anyone else and it was all getting too serious.

Up until that moment she'd always taken Jimmie for granted. But coming back to America after some months in England (travelling first class this time) it was much more difficult for them to avoid each other, and she was struck by everything he did. She noticed how popular he was with all the women and girls in the theatre, and became aware of how beautifully he played the piano. 'He could play nostalgic tunes by the hour. He'd go into the ship's music room and just play softly to himself. However, it always ended by people surrounding him and the girls were in the forefront around the piano,' she later recalled.

Annette had never been in such a situation before. Usually *she* was the object of admiration, a whole audience full of it. And the more persistent admirers would try to meet her. Except for the doctor she had been engaged to, such persistence never went any further. To them she would always be the Perfect Woman, an ethereal being with no faults. It was all very flattering and made her feel rather glamorous. With Jimmie it was different. He knew her as she really was, knew her better than she knew herself. 'That, as far as I can remember, took a little of the glamour away,' she wrote.

Their shipboard relations became considerably strained; they had been business partners for so long that they had no idea how to act with each other now that the relationship had changed. A sort of blanket embarrassment descended whenever they were together—Annette felt that she couldn't be coy with him like other girls because he knew her too well and Jimmie was constantly aware that he was just the paid manager and she was the star earning the big money. Jimmie had been in love with Annette for years, and had patiently kept it to himself until he could bear it no longer. For Annette, it was a much more recent discovery. They had reached a stalemate. She realised that Jimmie would never be able to work up the courage to court her, so she'd have to take the ball and run with it. But it wasn't as easy as she thought. She put it off from day to day until one day: 'After peeking through a porthole and seeing "Mister Sullivan" smiling so shyly at all the females, I made up my mind to act.'

For Annette, one of Jimmie's greatest charms was his smile. Writing over 30 years later, she said 'everybody from that day to this has always said "Oh hasn't Mr Sullivan got a lovely smile".' Never having had any reason to be jealous, Annette felt a strange pang when she saw Jimmie smiling at all those girls and guessed it was her first brush with the green-eyed monster.

As the oldest son of an Irish father and a German mother, Jimmie had grown up in a well-to-do suburb in Dubuque, Iowa. According to his niece, Virginia Gahlbeck, Jimmie had inherited the good looks of his mother: 'He was handsome with sparkling brown eyes.' His father, who was a good salesman but not a good businessman, died of a heart attack and left his wife and children almost penniless. Jimmie left school and went to work to support the family. By the time Annette met him, Jimmie had been working in carnivals and show business for almost four years and knew his way around. In a later letter Virginia Gahlbech said: 'He was handsome, charming, witty and aggressive, he had a way with people but he was also honest and dependable.' Jimmie and Annette had a lot in common; both still had the burden of supporting a family in reduced circumstances, and Jimmie's mother, though not a concert pianist like Annette's, was very accomplished and taught her eldest son how to play. Fortunately, Jimmie didn't inherit his father's lack of business acumen.

For a moment, Annette lost her confidence and could see all the reasons why they shouldn't marry—Jimmie hated exercise;

when he wasn't working, he was reading, he read everything in sight. And she was, of course, the complete opposite—she loved any form of exercise, never missed her 'physical jerks' every morning and always practised ballet at the *barre*. She loved being out and about driving the car or riding a horse. Perhaps there was no hope after all. She vacillated uncharacteristically until the last day on board, when she 'took the bull by the horns' and asked Jimmie to take a few rounds on the ship's deck. The first thing he said as they started was, 'Let's take it easy, I hate tramping around the deck.' Annette, feeling it was not going at all well, offered to sit it out in the deckchairs. As Annette herself put it:

> Real life isn't like books, I suppose, because we just sat there like a couple of dummies trying to make conversation. Finally, I gave up and we started for the Lounge door. In desperation I said, 'Oh Sweetheart!' Was my face red! I never saw anyone so flabbergasted. This is the true story of how Jimmie DID NOT propose to me.

There were no headlines this time. Mr and Mrs Sullivan kept it secret for weeks. They were married quietly in 1912 at Danbury, Connecticut while touring, on a one-night stand of all things— after the one show the town would see, they went to the local registry. However, theirs was definitely no one-night stand and, against all the odds facing a showbiz marriage, they stayed together for the rest for their lives. Annette always believed it worked out perfectly because they were so different. It was a classic example of opposites attracting. She loved having a nice quiet person to come home to after doing two shows a day. And later, as she began to experiment with different concepts in her act, Jimmie supported every one of her new-fangled ideas. For instance, when she took up wire walking in 1916, Annette observes in 'My Story' that:

> He didn't say: 'Listen you can't do that now you've grown up.'
> All he said was: 'It'll take a couple of years until you can really
> be any good at it—but go ahead.' Whatever I've tackled Jimmie
> always thought it was okay.

Jimmie, though smitten with Annette from the first moment they met, still had plenty to find out about her, 'At first her vivacious French temperament was a little hard to understand. We had our little squabbles like any other married pair, but I always knew when to keep quiet,' he said. 'It took time to grasp her untiring energy and ambition. When she made up her mind to undertake something, she really went after it and never let up.'

Even on their honeymoon Jimmie still couldn't quite believe she'd married *him*—a lazybones who hated 'to move a leg' unless he had to. When he finally worked up the courage to ask her why she'd consented to be his wife, she told him 'My word, Jimmie, thank heavens you're not a nut like me. Imagine both of us tearing around the universe practising and turning all sorts of somersaults from morning 'til night.'

Jimmie adjusted to Annette's lifestyle easily. He had enjoyed the night life, but once they were married they lived quietly and simply. As Jimmie observed, 'all invitations to nightclubs were strictly taboo—we just didn't care for them'. He came to prefer the life with Annette's friends whom he described as 'outdoor bugs'. Every summer they holidayed in France at Deauville, Dinard or on the Riviera.

Mipps, Annette's younger sister, remembered them in her memoirs, 'Let's Do Something', as a 'splendid and devoted team'. She believed that an artist needed a marriage of cooperation, and compared Annette and Jimmie's successful alliance to that of her parents, Frederick and Alice. Both Annette and Alice were creative, and they relied on the steadying influence of their respective husbands to achieve success. Annette realised how lucky she was: 'I want it understood that to my father and Jimmie I owe most of what success I've had,' she said in 'My Story'.

Frederick Kellerman had recognised very early on that Jimmie was, as his niece Virginia put it, 'a good kid'. Kellerman must have sensed that he was reliable and knew how to look after people. He had been doing it since he was sixteen.

Jimmie and Annette had a great mutual respect for each other, born of working together for so long before they were married. Jimmie recalled in the notes he wrote for the prospective screenplay of *Million Dollar Mermaid* in 1949, when they'd been married for 37 years, that in all that time:

> I can honestly say I never once heard Annette Kellerman have an angry word with anyone on stage or off. This is something of a record after years of trouping. Not that she was a Pollyanna. She hauled me over the coals enough if things were not just right with the show. That was one thing I learned.

And Jimmie, though quiet, could give as good as he got. 'When he gets angry,' Annette told reporter Vincent Flaherty in the 1950s, 'he says: "Any other man would have divorced you long ago".'

Mipps believed the secret to their successful marriage was that Jimmie had also learned who was the boss very early on in their relationship. Family friend June Smith was a child when she met Annette and Jimmie years later in the 1940s, during a stay in Sydney, and remembers that Annette always seemed to be in charge and was not always an easy guest. When they came to visit the family, Jimmie would always come in and sit straight down and play the piano, brilliantly. She recalled that Annette liked to have saccharine instead of sugar with her tea, she was still very figure-conscious, and that she would take a knife and cut the saccharine on the family's best cedar table. The marks are still there to this day. The Sullivans would come to visit in the early evening and when the clock struck seven Annette would say to her husband, no matter who else was talking, 'Jimmie, the news'. He would turn the radio on. Annette would then talk all the way through it, much to June's father's annoyance.

The marriage survived for 60 years, until Jimmie's death in 1972. Annette wrote: 'It takes two to make a marriage, with much give and take, but above all a sense of fair play is the basic idea.' Jimmie was for her 'a true partner, a real friend and the finest husband a woman ever had'.

As for Jimmie, Annette was always 'my only girl . . . We were separated once in our lives—business took us separate ways for about three weeks. The wastepaper basket was full of letters I wrote but didn't send . . . nuff said'.

9
SOME GREAT IDEAS FOR A MOVING PICTURE

Annette woke up at eight o'clock and, as usual, began her daily round of physical jerks which included working at the *barre* in the ballet studio at their house on the beach at Sheepshead Bay. This was as close to the sea as you could get in New York— right at the end of Ocean Avenue on Manhattan Beach Park and opposite Rockaway Beach and Queens. Annette had a bad feeling about her meeting with Mr Edward Albee, who was now the commander-in-chief of the Keith circuit. Since her return from England, she had begun touring again but the vaudeville circuit was changing. She had noticed other swimming acts on the bills posted up around town. Lifting her arms above her head and catching her reflection in the mirror, she examined her body objectively and was satisfied that she hadn't gained any pounds in London. But simply having kept the perfect figure wasn't going to stop others from copying her act. Once she had the monopoly on the title of Diving Venus, now they were everywhere. Even the Perfect Woman tag, though she'd always thought it was a little silly, was being claimed by others. A society debutante, Dorothy Ward, was insisting that her figure was more perfect than Annette's. She had managed to get the newspapers to print a ridiculous story promoting the idea of a 'duel of the tape measures' to prove it. Annette did an extra set of *pliés* and took a brisk walk before waking her husband. They'd been married only a few weeks and it still seemed a little strange that they were actually man and wife. Even though she'd known him all those years, she'd discovered so much more about Jimmie than she ever imagined—most amazing of all was that he'd never told her he couldn't swim. At first it was a little shocking, but now she didn't mind at all. They didn't need two swimmers in the family. After waking him up they would go and see what Mr Albee had to say for himself.

In 1912, Edward Albee was the most powerful man in vaudeville. The two independent theatre owners, William Morris and Morris Beck—the men who dared not fall in line or be swallowed up by the juggernaut of the all-encompassing Keith circuit—had been roundly dealt with by Albee. Performers were blacklisted if he even so much as suspected they were working for anyone else. He had successfully ruined the career of many a promising player. Beck and Morris were finding it more and more difficult to get anyone to play their theatres. Albee was not a man to be taken lightly. When Annette and Jimmie were ushered into his huge office on Broadway, he sat behind a massive mahogany desk smoking a large cigar. 'At ten o'clock in the morning!' thought Annette, horrified. After exchanging pleasantries about their recent wedding, Albee got straight to the point.

'Listen Annette, you've been with us for many years now and we think you should know that if you want any more dates we will have to lower your next season's salary,' he said.

He offered her $750 a week, half her normal salary. Annette sat there seething. She pointed out that the houses had been packed ever since she started working for Keith's.

'Well, we don't think you can do it again,' he said, chewing on his cigar and smiling.

'Well, Mr Albee,' Annette said getting to her feet, 'it looks as though your circuit owes me nothing and therefore I owe you nothing.'

She told him she would definitely not be signing up at that salary and if he ever wanted her act again they would have to pay $2500 a week. With that she took Jimmie's hand, turned and walked out.

It is interesting that Jimmie, though present at the meeting, never opened his mouth. Annette always saw herself as the big star and him as 'the silent partner'. He was a quiet, efficient man and liked being in the background, hating to have his photo taken. The only snapshots of him are with Annette and a group of other young people when they were young and carefree on Brighton Beach, New York in 1909. There's another picture of them standing on the steps of the registry office in Danbury, Connecticut, Annette holding a bouquet of flowers with a cheeky dimpled smile and Jimmie staring back a little suspiciously at the camera. A later photo taken in the 1950s shows Jimmie and Annette grinning. He is sitting and she is standing behind him with her arms crossed on his shoulders. They look happy, but it's obvious who's the boss.

When she was writing her life story for the film *Million Dollar Mermaid*, Jimmie asked Annette to mention him as little as possible, but what glimpses there are reveal someone with a strong will of his own, especially in a crisis. At dramatic points in his wife's career, Jimmie was always there to take control and calm things down, and at the time of her vaudeville successes he was acknowledged by the press: 'Either Annette Kellerman is the greatest box office attraction the stage has ever known or else her manager is the most compelling genius of modern theatrical achievement, and the writer is inclined to the belief that both statements apply.' They were definitely a team.

When Annette left Keith's, Jimmie was totally in favour of the move. She had felt frustrated for some time by the fact that she was always described as a diver, or a mermaid, or the Perfect Woman. She wanted to show the public that she was 'not just a pretty fish'. For a long time she'd had an idea which could only be realised through the medium of motion pictures—an underwater fairlytale or, as she described it in 'My Story', a 'water movie with mermaids'.

At first no one, not even Jimmie, was convinced by the idea. He pointed out that pantomimes were all very well in England, but they would never work in America. 'This is a hard-boiled country,' he told her. However, he agreed to go with her and do the rounds of the movie studios.

By 1912 the movie business was flourishing. Though the 1920s and 1930s are usually perceived as the era when the great movie moguls began to dominate the scene, the Hollywood of the early teens had already established the blueprint of the system that was to remain in place until the 1950s. Large studios like Universal and Fox were thriving. And they were run by hard-nosed businessmen with more interest in big bucks than big ideas. Annette and Jimmie's attempts to sell their mermaid fantasy met with absolutely no success.

'Can't you see beautiful water scenes with mermaids and sirens?' Annette asked Harry Aitken, who distributed Charlie Chaplin and D.W. Griffith.

'No,' he replied bluntly. 'Women always look like drowned rats to me when they come out of the water.'

When he, in turn, suggested Annette star in a comedy, she told him straight out: 'My idea is a much better one. Just you wait and see.'

Discouraged by the whole experience, the Sullivans went out with friends that night. Annette was seated next to Captain Leslie T. Peacock. The Captain, if that was his real title, was one in a long line of Englishmen who had come to Hollywood and reinvented themselves—a list that included Chaplin, Douglas Fairbanks and Archie Leach, the cockney youth who became the sophisticated Cary Grant. Captain Leslie T. Peacock (who was always mentioned by his full name) had moved from being a writer of popular romances in magazines to become a well-known screenplay writer, known to have some considerable influence down at Universal. When Annette told him about her idea for a movie set in Neptune's garden, he was enthusiastic. He asked her to tell him the story in detail and was so impressed he went straight home and wrote a draft of *Neptune's Daughter* that same night.

The next day Peacock arranged an interview with Carl Lemmle, who was running Universal Studios at the time, warning her that they would have a battle on their hands. He explained that nothing like *Neptune's Daughter* had been done on the screen before and, to realise their idea, Universal would have to spend more money on it than any other picture ever produced.

As the Captain predicted, the interview was stormy. Like everyone else they had approached, Carl Lemmle hated the idea. 'What!' he exclaimed with a look of distaste. 'A woman fish on screen!'

It's here that Annette's writings give us a rare glimpse of Jimmie Sullivan, the manager, in action. He pointed out to Lemmle that Annette had come to America with a brand new stage show and had repeatedly packed theatres from coast to coast. He reminded him how she had lectured to thousands of women and given the world the one-piece bathing suit. He told Lemmle that Annette's ideas were popular, up to date and often ahead of their time. Making this movie would afford him the opportunity to present the phenomenon known as Annette Kellerman in a whole new way. Lemmle took the bait, but with reservations.

'I think you have an idea,' he told Jimmie, 'but if this is a failure, heaven help you, Jimmie Sullivan.'

Carl Lemmle's bark was far worse than his bite, Annette described him as 'a dear old man' and found the experience of making *Neptune's Daughter* by far the most pleasant of her whole movie-making career.

The film was assigned Universal's ace young director, Herbert Brenon. He had already directed 37 films in the last two years, but nothing on the scale of *Neptune's Daughter*. Like Peacock, he was English, which pleased Annette because she appreciated the English tradition of pantomime and their abiding preoccupation with the supernatural—even the creator of Sherlock Holmes, Arthur Conan Doyle, believed in fairies at the bottom of the garden. The American dream was a far more material one. Brenon was talented, quick-witted and ambitious. He immediately fell out with Peacock because he took over the script and claimed it as his own. Annette and Herbert had much in common; they were around the same age and both had worked in vaudeville. They were eager to make a mark with this reworking of a classic myth from the waters of the Aegean, transplanting it from the old world to the new Hollywood dream factory. Despite the fact that Brenon claimed credit for direction, production and writing, the film was definitely a team effort between the two of them.

'Every time he got stuck for something,' Annette recalled many years later, 'he'd say to me "What do think we should do here?"'

Annette made suggestions about the storyline, the locations and what stunts she would perform. And, when she became more familiar with the technicalities of movie-making, she began to suggest how scenes should be shot. She was as much a creative force as her director or any of the technicians involved. The only other movie stars at the time to have comparable control over their films were Mary Pickford, the most powerful woman working in Hollywood at the time, Charlie Chaplin and Douglas Fairbanks.

The film was made on location in Bermuda. No passenger ships were travelling there, so Universal hired a cargo boat to take the cast and crew over to film in the pristine forests and underground caves that abounded there. Bermuda was still a sleepy little colony, unknown to most of the world—a rather exotic place, strange and beautiful enough to imagine its tropical seas might be peopled by mermaids. For audiences of the day, especially in small-town America where the average person had never seen New York, let alone Bermuda, *Neptune's Daughter* was the most amazing spectacle they would ever behold. As a delightful water sprite, Annette dances about freely and nearly naked in a tiny piece of diaphanous fabric, is then captured and bound, and pushed over a cliff; yet she emerges, Houdini-like, to fight like a man and save the prince. While other movie heroines swooned at the slightest provocation, Annette cast aside all encumbrances as she cut a swathe through the hapless villains of the piece—Hollywood's first-ever swashbuckling heroine.

And she did literally everything, refusing to use a double. It was against her principles. In one scene she was required to fight with the villain on a cliff's edge; then, locked in combat, they would plunge off the edge together. Unable to find an actor who could also swim, Brenon volunteered. Annette said in a 1975 interview that she told him she hoped he was a good swimmer, 'because I didn't want to have to pull him out'. Like most of the stunts in the film, this daredevil leap had not been tried before. It seems that Brenon and Annette were equally brave or foolish. Though neither of them really knew what they were doing, they were willing to try anything to make a better picture. In this case, the whole stunt almost ended in disaster. The *Baltimore News* reported:

> As both fell, Mr Brenon's head struck Miss Kellerman's temple. To the astonishment of hundreds of spectators, she rose to the surface quite unconscious. It took but a few seconds to realise she was seriously hurt; a boat nearby, manned by Mr Sullivan and Mr Hooper, Mr Brenon's assistant, quickly came to the spot and the plucky little woman was pulled into the boat. She recovered shortly.

After being dragged unconscious from the water, Annette was back at work bright and early the next day. It is impossible to imagine a movie star of today being quite so cooperative.

According to the script, after they fell off the cliff, the fight between the villain and the heroine continued underwater. This scene was to be shot in a glass-fronted tank about 16 feet square. The glass was three-quarters of an inch thick, even though Annette and Brenon had requested glass $1\frac{1}{2}$ inches thick. A covered canvas passageway was built up to the sides of the glass front and blankets covered the walls so no light could get in. People were rushing in and out of the passage getting ready for the scene, bringing rocks and seaweed for the background. Finally, a large turtle and a variety of different fish were dumped into the 5000 gallons of water in the tank. Brenon seemed to be everywhere directing the action. Annette was pacing up and down the beach nervously, her arms folded. They had been reassured that the glass in the tank was safe, but neither Annette nor Brenon was convinced. In the event that something might go wrong, Jimmie and Brenon's assistant Hooper had bound their hands in hessian bagging and had taken up positions on either side of the camera ready to save the actors. Walter H. Bernard, reporter from *Motion Picture Magazine,* was on the set at the time and reported on the filming of the scene in July 1914:

> Brenon and Miss Kellerman, in their costumes, which, by the way, were very scanty, exposing much of their naked bodies, prepared to climb the ladder and get into the tank. We just held our breath as they slowly slid into the water. Nothing happened. They grew bolder, rehearsed the scene and six pictures were taken of it. We could hear the buzzing of the camera as the crank turned.

When they came up for air, after having done the takes, Jimmie was adamant they stop: 'Come on out now! You've got all the scenes you want—this tank won't hold much longer!'

Annette, egged on by Brenon, wanted to do one more take. 'I'm sure we can make the next one better,' she said. Walter Bernard continues his eyewitness account:

> We saw them take a deep breath and once more go under the water. Hardly had they disappeared when there was a 'Boom!' like the echo of a firing cannon and immediately the canvas passage was swept away and tons of water rushed thru [*sic*] the smashing glass. It carried with it the bodies of Miss Kellerman and Mr Brenon, fish, rocks, turtle and everything else the tank

had contained and swept the photographer, Hooper and Sullivan off their feet and mixed them up with the rest. The precautions taken by Sullivan and Hooper were useless. Everything including actors, photographers, assistants and scenery had been wiped away completely as if by magic. Our hearts jumped into our mouths as we thought of the fate of poor Miss Kellerman and Mr Brenon. Their bodies lay motionless among the wreckage. They were shockingly cut and bleeding and we thought them surely dead.

Fortunately both survived, though Annette was cut badly on the right leg and foot. Brenon, however, was much more seriously injured. 'He looked as if someone had chopped him all over with a hatchet,' Annette wrote later in *How to Swim*. He was badly slashed around his face and neck, and his left arm, which was sliced open from his shoulder to his wrist, required 46 stitches.

A photo taken at the time showed that the hole in the tank, through which they were sucked, was only just large enough for a person to crawl through. While Brenon had panicked and fought against the rush of the water, Annette, feeling as comfortable underwater as in air, had remained calm, instinctively rolling up into a ball and letting herself run with it. However, she remained in hospital for six weeks, one week longer than Brenon, because the wound on her foot was too close to the bone to stitch and wouldn't heal. It left a bad scar, but Annette was just grateful she wasn't cut on her face or her body. As soon as they recovered both returned to the set, Brenon on crutches, ready to complete the movie.

Even before it was released, *Neptune's Daughter* was the talk of the town and Annette and Brenon the heroes of the moment.

'Do you mean to say,' a friend of Walter Bernard's asked him at the time, 'that those two people, knowing that the tank would probably break, and that they would be cut to death, dared deliberately to climb in there?'

'Certainly,' he replied. 'It was part of the work and they never even complained.'

Three months later, the film opened at the Globe Theatre in New York, marking 'the entry of another Broadway theatre into the ranks of Broadway playhouses that are now given over to this form of entertainment,' reported the New York Review. Ironically, vaudeville theatres and the genre itself, the entertainment form that Annette loved most, were being overtaken by the medium she had the least respect for—movies. 'I never wanted to be a picture star,' she said later to Joel Greenberg. 'I liked the movement of the theatre.'

Neptune's Daughter, the film that 'nobody concerned had any faith in', opened on 25 April 1914 and played at the Globe Theatre to capacity houses for the next seven months. It had cost the sceptical Lemmle $35 000 and was to make him and Universal Studios over a million. Its record of nineteen weeks of packed houses finally fell in 1955 when This is Cinerama was released.

Across the country the reviews were consistently fantastic. In New York it was: 'The finest picture ever shown'. In Atlanta it was described as, 'The biggest film feature that has ever come south'. In Chicago, where people remembered her from the ten cent pavilion, her vaudeville act had not been as successful as elsewhere in the country, but Neptune's Daughter caused a commotion. Downtown Michigan Avenue displayed a carnival atmosphere when several thousand well-dressed people congregated outside the Fine Arts Theatre. 'Squads of police were present to conserve decorum and counsel patience,' said the Chicago Tribune. Patrons waited for hours in double lines around the block to get a ticket. The *Chicago Tribune* reported that: 'Every once in while a young woman attendant would appear at the entrance and lift a symbolic hand—if two places were available two fingers would be raised and two of the waiters would be admitted.'

In July business was still brisk and showed no signs of slowing. After screening for only two months, 70 000 Chicagoans had seen *Neptune's Daughter*. It was the same in every town all over the country—the film's season was constantly being extended. Audiences were returning to see the film over and over again. 'Never before in the annals of picturedom has a film created such a furore,' was the enthusiastic verdict of the *Pittsburgh Leader*.

Even though the 'annals of picturedom' did not stretch back that far, audiences were by now accustomed to the cinema as a form of popular entertainment. However, technical changes were happening so fast, comparable in many ways to the leaps and bounds made in today's digital technology, that audiences of 1912 would have been thrilled at the advances made in *Neptune's Daughter* when it was released just two years later. It was a big-budget picture for those days, and employed very advanced camera work. But the attraction for most people seemed to be, as Annette had predicted, the novelty of a fairytale realised on screen.

The story was simple. Annette, daughter of Neptune, swears revenge when her young mermaid sister is captured in a fisherman's net and dies. She is transformed by the Sea Witch into a mortal and is determined to kill the Land King who took her sister. She falls in love with the King, who is disguised as a humble peasant, and when she later discovers his true identity at a Royal Ball, she cannot fulfil her mission. Broken-hearted, she returns to the sea but pines so much that her father sends her back to the Land and the King she loves.

Before *Neptune's Daughter*, a fairytale was something you read in a book with pretty illustrations. Suddenly, audiences were seeing real mermaids swimming and diving in exotic locations. Somehow, seeing it up there on the big screen made it alright for adults as well as children to indulge in their passion for fairytales. There was also the allure of seeing, for the first time, a film which was set underwater. The *Buffalo Times* wrote:

> It was demonstrated to the lovers of the 'movies' that it is possible to take real motion pictures underwater. Of course, there have been pictures showing fish and other living things of the deep but pictures showing real human beings underwater have hitherto been considered impossible.

The incredible success of the film surprised even Annette. She felt a new confidence in her abilities as an actress and, once back in the theatre, wanted to show them off. She was no longer interested in a simple display of her physical prowess. 'I'm tired of flopping into tanks full of the water supply of strange cities,' she told the *Detroit News*. 'I really am an actress and I enjoyed acting in *Neptune's Daughter*, even if there is a lot of swimming in it, because this trained seal stuff gets on one's nerves.'

It seemed that Keith's circuit still wanted a trained seal, and Annette was not willing to comply. She was prouder of the film than anything else she'd ever done. At last she felt she had made something really artistic, something her mother—her ideal of a true artiste—would appreciate. Though both were performers, their careers had taken very different paths. Alice, with the support of her family, had been able to pursue her dream of becoming a concert pianist and composer. Annette had to support her family and abandon her dreams of a serious acting career. *Neptune's Daughter* changed all that. Not only was she an actress on screen, but she had worked behind the scenes to make her idea come to life. It was always her favourite movie. Even in her late eighties, she was still telling interviewers: 'The best work I ever did was in *Neptune's Daughter*.'

Annette decided to leave America and return to Paris, taking with her 50 negatives of her picture to show to her mother. The film hadn't been released in France. Despite the movie's rave reviews and incredible popularity, it was Alice Kellerman's approval that Annette really craved. She had planned to stay away to study singing for two years to star in a musical, *The Mermaid* written for her by Captain Peacock. It was a serious move. She sold her interest in the film back to Universal for a huge $30 000, and actually did study singing under Melba for a short time in Paris. The plan was to make her debut in *The Mermaid* in Australia and return triumphant to the Broadway stage as a fully-fledged musical comedy star. 'America will not see Miss Kellerman again for two long and, to *Vanity Fair*, weary years,' bemoaned one sentimental journalist.

When she and Jimmy arrived in Paris, things didn't go according to plan. Mipps, Maurice, Frederick Jnr and Alice were living in the house Annette had bought them with her savings from White City and Wonderland. It was an imposing three-storey, eighteenth century townhouse with double cedar doors and a wide entrance staircase, set in a large garden in suburban Rueil Malmaison, not too far from Versailles. Annette was greeted by a worn-out Mipps who told her she had just been stepping out to cable her. Annette knew their mother was very sick, though Madame Kellerman herself had not been told of the extreme severity of her condition. She lay propped up on her pillows, her once round, pink-cheeked face now hollow and pale. Annette, suppressing her distress at her mother's appearance, kept up the jolly façade of a normal holiday visit. She had last seen Alice Kellerman four years before when she was fit and well and had been presented with the honours of the *Instruction Publique* for forming a conservatoire in Australia and for her compositions. Annette, Mipps and her brothers took turns by Alice's bedside. Annette showed her mother the stills and was thrilled at her reaction. She told her about the beautiful music written for the film and its huge success in America. 'It was a moment of great pride in my career,' she wrote in 'My Story', 'that I had proved to my mother that I had inherited some of her great artistry.'

Alice Charbonnet Kellerman died a few days later. Annette, heartbroken, stayed in Paris a little longer, studying singing and dancing, but the city was not the same without her mother. She cut short her stay and returned to America. As soon as she arrived in New York she was summoned to the offices of Edward Albee. She refused to go in person and sent her New York theatrical agent, who returned with the news of a contract for the $2500 a week she had asked for at their last meeting. The contract was on her terms. She wasn't going back to be a trained seal any longer. Annette completely changed her act. There was a ballet number done on *pointe* shoes called *The Peacock* (surely named in gratitude to the Captain), followed by a comedy routine. Finally, there was the new glass-fronted tank that allowed the audience to enjoy the spectacle as she dived underwater in a beautiful full-length red bathing suit, her every movement dramatically lit. She was happy to be back treading the boards, and the show proved to be so popular it toured the country for the next two years. But Hollywood had not forgotten *Neptune's Daughter* or her extraordinary success. It wanted Annette back—at any price.

10
MILLION DOLLAR MOVIE

Daughter of the Gods! We're in thy debt!
Annette, Annette!
To conquer weakness nor to frette,
Until each obstacle was mette
Thy triumph, dear, is one safe bette!
Annette! Annette!

Motion Picture Magazine, June 1917

On a cold January day in 1915, down at the cargo docks in New York City, workers witnessed an unusual scene. A group of well-dressed people, the sort you might see travelling first class on an ocean liner, were climbing up the rickety ramp of the rusty old fruit steamer bound for Jamaica. At the top a woman could be seen holding up all the rest of the cast and crew members; she stopped and turned, displaying her figure to its best advantage, tightly clad in a velvet dress of the very latest fashion, for the camera men who clustered around her. The dock workers recognised Annette Kellerman and gathered around to catch a glimpse of the star of *Neptune's Daughter*—a little disappointed that she was not as scantily attired as they had seen her on the big screen.

On the strength of *Neptune's Daughter* William Fox was planning even greater but stardom for Annette. She, Jimmie, Herbert Brenon and a huge cast and crew were off to make a cinematic spectacle that would rival Griffith's *Intolerance* and *Birth of a Nation*. They were expecting to be in Jamaica for two to three months at most—but Annette would not see New York for another nine months.

On her return from Paris Annette had planned to stay in vaudeville, but was persuaded by William Fox to do another picture with Herbert Brenon.

In 1915, making the move from vaudeville to movies and back again was not at all unusual. Most people in the entertainment industry had a foot in each camp. The film industry was located in New York, with the main studios situated at Fort Lee in New Jersey. The tycoons running the movie industry also, more often than not, were still the magnates of vaudeville. From 1907 onwards, directors used the Pallisades near Fort Lee as a background for the popular new Wild West movies. It was here that D.W. Griffith, shooting one of his earliest movies, made the first sophisticated use of the technique of cross-cutting, or the cutback, to build tension. Instead of the usual long, slow scenes, Griffith cut between scenes much faster so the audience saw, for instance, an innocent girl picking flowers in a sunny field one second and the next her evil nemesis stalking the shadowy streets, drunken and angry in search of her.

When there were any studio shots to do be done, Annette would simply catch the ferry over from New York to New Jersey. At the time there were fifteen different studios in and around Fort Lee, including Fox, Universal and Metro. It was a smaller and much more intimate setting than the big conglomerate of studios that Hollywood would end up becoming. Everyone knew everyone else. Fox rented two large studios, which resembled twin glass barns, from 'Doc' Willat. This remained Fox's principal studio until production was shifted to New York City and Los Angeles in 1919.

Here Annette met everyone from Buster Keaton to Gloria Swanson, Charlie Chaplin to Erich Von Stroheim. 'At that time Hollywood was not the Hollywood it became. Everybody was just scratching for bread and butter,' Annette told interviewer Joel Greenberg, many years later. 'If they were in a Fox film they were lucky. Those were the days before everyone got too high hat and got to the drink. There were no special stars.'

She loved Buster Keaton, recalling that he used to call her Anne and promised they would make a movie together one day. Before they could, Keaton made an unfortunate marriage and then, as Annette mentioned matter-of-factly to Joel Greenberg: 'He lost his head and drank and went to the dogs.' She wasn't so keen on Cecil B. de Mille—'he was very much taken up with his girls'—but she liked his brother. Lon Chaney was okay and Will Rogers was 'an awfully nice chap' with whom she would often go out riding. She didn't care for Douglas Fairbanks much at all.

It was an exciting time for the movie industry, as the demands of making almost every film necessitated the invention of some innovative hardware or new technique, and no one knew from week to week what was going to happen next. Camera men who invented a new gadget for their camera one week were millionaires the next. Two, whom Annette worked with on *Neptune's Daughter* and *A Daughter of the Gods*, became millionaires when their inventions for film cameras were bought and patented at this time.

In less than twenty years film had grown from kinescope machines, the short one-reel movies which could be watched by only one viewer, to nickelodeons. Named for the ticket price of one nickel, these were storefront theatres, bare rooms with a sheet for a screen, a few benches and a box for collecting admission, hence the term 'box office'. Lower and middle-class customers went to the nickelodeons, but by the time *Neptune's Daughter* was completed in 1914, big-time vaudeville managers were dividing the program between live acts and movies, and attracting the more respectable middle- and upper middle-class customers. When William Fox decided to invest in *A Daughter of the Gods,* the first of the big-budget blockbusters were just beginning to be made. Rather than just a series of images, the cinema was embracing the narrative form. The bar was raised considerably upon the release of D.W. Griffth's twelve-reel saga, *Birth of a Nation,* in 1915.

Movie moguls saw the tremendous popularity of film in the growth of specially designed theatres for them. The first motion picture palace in America, The Regent, opened in 1913 and was quickly followed by a succession of opulent theatres along Broadway.

William Fox, with fellow Hungarian Adolf Zukor, was one of the first movie moguls to emerge at this time. He had spent years in theatre and vaudeville, and was canny enough to see in 1914, when he started his own studio, that movies were here to stay and there was plenty of money to be made for anyone willing to invest.

After *Neptune's Daughter,* Fox lured Herbert Brenon away from Universal. By the time Annette had signed up to make *A Daughter of the Gods,* Brenon had already directed two movies for Fox with Theda Bara. She was the star who really put Fox studios on the map and gave a whole new meaning to the word 'vampire'— she was the very first Hollywood 'vamp'. Making more than

40 motion pictures within three years, mostly costume spectacles, she played irresistible, heartless women who lived only for sensual pleasure. Her name, invented by the studio, was an anagram of 'Arab Death'. Her films set the vogue for sophisticated sexual themes in motion pictures and made her an international symbol of daring new freedom. She and Valaska Surrat, another successful 'vamp', were Fox's two biggest stars. In her late eighties, Annette could still recall that first meeting with Fox and Brenon. She told interviewer Joel Greenberg: 'All he and Fox thought about was Theda Bara. She was a nice sort of a soul, she wasn't much. She looked like a siren.'

When Jimmie and the non-drinking, non-smoking very *un*vamp-like Annette met Fox, she told Greenberg: 'He treated us like imbeciles.' Her idea for a big budget film set in Arabia and in the Kingdom of Mermaids seemed ridiculous to Fox. However, Brenon, who by this time had gained Fox's trust and admiration, persuaded the tycoon that this film would be bigger and better than anything D.W. Griffiths would do. Fox was successfully convinced and guaranteed Herbert Brenon as much money as he needed. 'He was Fox's little baby,' Annette later said of Brenon. 'He [Fox] would do anything for him.'

The preparations had begun over six months before the cast and crew left for Jamaica. One of the first things Annette and Brenon had to do was find mermaids—200 of them. The audition was held at Dr Savage's 'natatorium' in West 29th Street, New York. The poolside was packed with journalists dressed in their Sunday best, not minding the splashes of various would-be mermaids as they demonstrated their style. They all came early for once and remained till late to cover their assignment. As one reporter from *Motion Picture Magazine* put it: 'Wherever the eye wandered, on the surface of the water, under the water or languidly basking in the warm air' there were girls of all shapes and sizes hoping to qualify as sirens. While Annette judged their aquatic skills, Brenon 'cast an appraising eye over their physical contours'. Most of the girls were not skilled swimmers or divers. Annette would have to spend weeks in Jamaica training them to swim, and then teach them how to make their way through the water with their legs tied together so that once they had their tails attached they would swim like mermaids.

When the cast and crew finally arrived in Jamaica and all was ready to begin, the film was nearly over before it had even started. Annette had brought with her Coo-ee—Coodles for short—her adored little black pug. When they disembarked in Kingston they were greeted by the stiff upper-lipped colonial governor, Sir William Manning, who took one look at the dog and ordered it off the island: 'The inhabitants of Jamaica fear rabies more than they fear the wrath of God.' Annette was indignant. 'Well,' she told him, 'there ain't going to be no picture.' If the dog couldn't stay, neither would she. It seemed the stand-off would continue until the captain of an oil tanker anchored in the bay offered to take the dog and also to provide an offshore berth for Jimmie and Annette. Annette took up the generous invitation and abandoned the luxuries of the Jamaican Hotel. 'It was a case of Mahomet and the mountain. Since Cooie [*sic*] might not go to Miss Kellerman, the wondrously formed Annette went to Cooie. Mr and Mrs James Sullivan's Jamaican address was the malodourous steamship,' reported the *New York Star*.

And so it was that for the next nine months Coodles never again set paw upon land. Annette remembered coming home after a hard day in the water or riding down a dangerous mountain and hearing the reassuring bark of her treasured companion as he heard them approach. Annette, who never had children, loved her dogs and Coo-ee seems to have been a particular favourite. There are numerous photos of her and the dog in newspapers of the time. In her late eighties she could still recount tales of Coo-ee as if he were a person.

There's no mention in 'My Story' of why Annette never had children. When she was first starring on the New York vaudeville stage she mentioned more than once that she wanted a family. But it was almost impossible in those days to be a mother and have a career. Though she advised married women on how to exercise to retain their figures after childbirth, Annette may, like Scarlet O'Hara, have feared the effect of childbearing on her own physique. Then again, her sister Mipps had no children either. The reasons why were simply not spoken about by their generation.

Once Coo-ee and her mistress were settled on the oil tanker, Annette was ready to start work. She began training 150 New York girls to be mermaids. She then had to organise 1200 Jamaican children under the age of seven into an orderly group. First they had to be fitted with their costumes—white beards, pointed caps and little green outfits. They were to play the residents of the Gnome Kingdom where she flees after being hounded out of town by a salacious sultan who is after more than just Anitia's mind. It is testament to the extent of her popularity and fame that, in all her films, apart from *What Women Love*, Annette's characters were either called Annette or something close to it, like Anitia.

The Gnome Village was built in miniature by 60 carpenters and masons in a pristine wilderness region of Jamaica known as the Roaring River Falls. Hidden away in one of the most inaccessible parts of the island, its potential was discovered by the expert eyes of those in the 'decorating department'.

A Daughter of the Gods set the standard for the tradition of the impermanent imperialism of big-budget Hollywood film shoots. The film crew would arrive, taking over and changing not only the location but the entire landscape and the local economy for the term of the film's production. Just as suddenly, like a colonial power, they would strategically withdraw, leaving the country bereft of patronage. Because most of the world had been discovered and colonised by 1915, directors, behaving like true imperialists, went to exotic locations and made their own worlds in which, for the duration of the shoot, they were absolute rulers. In the case of *A Daughter of the Gods* Brenon persuaded Fox to lease an entire island for the duration and, according to the *Evening Wisconsin*, 'placed the entire population under salary'.

For the construction of the Gnome Kingdom, Brenon hired 300 native workers to 'clear away every obstruction' in the virgin rainforest. Their task was to dump a hundred cartloads of sand and clay at the bottom of a picturesque waterfall for the sole purpose of providing a light foreground. Masons and builders were brought in to construct hundreds of little huts. A miniature village sprang up almost overnight, with little churches, public squares and winding streets. When it was ready, the children were brought in and divided into groups, each with a supervisor. While not in the water the mermaids doubled as gnome nannies. Annette, known to the children as 'the pretty lady', came in and oversaw the running of the whole village and the training of the gnomes. She said in a *Detroit News* article:

> We engaged the children from babes-in-arms up to seven years old. They were to receive a shilling per day, and to each child who brought a donkey went an extra one. They were the dearest kiddies I have ever seen.

She set up a fairytale school where the children were read the stories and legends of other countries and were then examined to see how much they had understood. By the time shooting began the Jamaican children had a comprehensive knowledge of the European gnome. Annette thought of everything and everyone—when some of the parents proved anxious about having their children in the care of strangers for months at a time, she had special quarters built for them to stay and paid them to take time off from their labours to be near their children. A hospital was built on location and staffed by doctors and nurses. Annette was so popular with the children, the *Detroit News* reported, that when the script called for the gnomes to attack her, they refused en masse. 'It took the longest time to make them realise that they must whip me and push me and when they finally decided it was alright, they did so, but with no heart in the task.'

Annette was involved with the film at all levels. Not only did she train the mermaids for two months, she also found the right fabric for their tails. She and Brenon scoured the wholesale houses in New York for the appropriate material. When they found it, they ordered 10 000 metres and had it shipped to Jamaica where the tails were made up by the costume department under the supervision of Mrs Irene Lee, who had 150 000 sewing machines and 20 000 extras to costume. The fabric didn't last long in the tropical Jamaican waters, so every ten days duplicates had to be made.

In between shooting the picture, Annette managed to enjoy the social life of the island, as an article in *Motion Picture Classic* describes:

. . . riding her black horse Pluto amid the luxuriant tropical foliage to King's House, home of the Governor, Sir William

Manning. At the tennis courts near Rose Gardens, she held her own against crack tennis players. And then there was many an early morning jaunt across Kingston Harbour with the beautiful Miss Kellerman at the helm of the yacht or guiding the swift motor boat which conveyed the principles [*sic*] of the company.

Then, of course, there were the stunts. The unprecedented scale of the film challenged Annette to come up with something even more dangerous and daring than she'd ever done before. The script that Brenon and she had collaborated on called for her to dive off a waterfall, handcuffed and ankle-locked, but Fox wasn't willing to risk his star. According to the *Toledo Blade*, when Annette received her copy of the script there were blue lines through the scene. She protested the cuts to Fox, who told her: 'It sounds entirely too dangerous to me, and besides the map of the island doesn't show a waterfall.'

'That's the way,' she replied. 'Somebody's always trying to take the joy out of life.'

Fox then pressed a button and his stenographer entered.

'How high do you want your Niagara, Miss Kellerman?' Fox asked humbly.

'Oh about 60 feet,' she announced.

Then to his stenographer: 'Cablegram, Fox's engineers Jamaica: provide beautiful 60 foot waterfall.'

Over in Jamaica the engineers immediately set to work and diverted the course of a river to create a picturesque cascade above the tiny gnome village. The only problem was that, although Annette was not worried about having her hands and ankles tied, she was a little daunted when she saw the waterfall and the rapids below, and wanted to take a little time to work herself up to it. Brenon, who was keen to film the scene, decided to try a dog first (a Jamaican dog, not Coo-ee). The unfortunate mongrel was thrown over but never emerged from the churning rapids below. Brenon sent a native Jamaican down to see what had happened, but he could find nothing. They were about to abandon the idea when they heard barking echoing through the valley and the dog was found safe and sound in a cave. Brenon, encouraged, wanted to shoot the scene before it got dark. Annette, standing uncertainly on the cliff's edge for a second, suddenly took a deep breath and dived off, plunging into the heart of the rapids where she was swept out to sea. The current from the artificial waterfall was strong and Annette, hands still tied, could see that she was heading straight for the jagged rocks lining the shoreline but could do little to stop herself being dashed against them. Somehow she grabbed hold of a rock and, Houdini-esque, cut the binding cords on its sharp edges. The film crew watched in awe from the waterfall and were relieved to see her emerge safe, though covered in blood, which was flowing from her wrists. She had survived, but only just, having almost severed her arteries in the process.

Other stunts, equally perilous, didn't seem to bother her as much. To escape the Sheik, Anitia, locked away at the top of his tower, had to climb out the cell window and dive 105 feet down over treacherous rocks into the Caribbean. In another scene she had to lead the gnome army down a precipitous slope. She described the experience many years later:

> I rode ahead of them. We had to come down a gorge to the
> bottom and when I think of it now I must have been mad. If
> I'd taken two steps the wrong way I would have been over the
> precipice. It never struck me that I was doing anything silly.
> I had no sense of danger, I really didn't.

Later she had to fall in full armour from her horse into the sea and then scramble out of the suit and continue to fight the enemy. The one scene that did leave a mark, not physically but emotionally, was the crocodile scene. It was pivotal also to the relationship between Brenon, herself and Jimmie.

Brenon and Annette were in many ways well matched. Both were charismatic and athletic. Though, like Jimmie, he was a small man, Brenon made up for his lack of height with his charm and Irish good looks—he had blue eyes, soft wavy brown hair and an impish, slightly upturned nose. He was the quintessential stereotype of the Hollywood director, commanding huge sums of money and the services of thousands of people. Through the long months of shooting in the forest, he hired a native band to keep up the spirits of the Jamaican extras, shot 44 miles of film and built a refrigerating plant to keep it cool. He collected 2500 horses, 2000 cattle, 800 sheep, 1000 donkeys, 500 miscellaneous animals, 2000 lizards, fourteen swans, ten camels and a flock of sparrows from New York. He was one of the first directors to shoot with seven cameras. Like Annette, he was popular with the cast and crew, letting them put baby sharks in his bathtub and not losing his temper in the tropical heat. He also gave a concert and raised $3500 for the British Red Cross. He drove his people relentlessly from dawn until dusk, yet from Annette down to the lowliest roustabout he managed to keep the loyal friendship of all. Coming from a wealthy Irish family, he was eccentric, and although he was married, he never took his wife on location, instead taking his mother and consulting her on every particular of the movie.

Brenon was also the opposite of Jimmie. Annette never mentioned it, but there must have been friction between the two men. Throughout the nine months of filming, Jimmie was almost always there, even though he refused to take a wage. Annette and Brenon spent every waking moment together. For weeks they trekked for miles through the jungle with the cameraman, scouting locations and planning scenes. 'We'd go out on these long treks . . . I was a stickler for that. I used to go anywhere if it was going to be a beautiful shot. We did some beautiful, beautiful things,' she said in an interview. Annette's favourite location was one where she had to swing out from a tree and dive into a pool below. Annette's sister Mipps later said in 'Let's Do Something' that the tree to which the swing was attached was '60 foot high with tropical vines and liana curling and climbing all the way, shadows and sun peeping through'.

Jimmie must have felt a little left out. At one point, to keep him busy, he was detailed to collect crocodiles for a new scene— probably inserted by Brenon, though in the subsequent fallout nobody admitted authorship. He had to drive to the other side of the island with a party of natives and shoot, but not kill, crocodiles. Rough truck journeys, which were killing too many of these unfortunate reptiles, meant further arduous trapping trips back and forth across the island. Once they had enough crocodiles, Jimmie had to look after them, making sure that there were no dogs anywhere nearby as the smell or sight of them sent the crocs berserk.

The scene they were to be used in was when the Sheik declares that Anitia is a sorceress and decides to punish her by having his two most powerful eunuchs throw her into a pool full of slavering, open-mouthed crocodiles. Jimmie was led to believe that a dummy was to be thrown to the crocs, not his wife. Despite his anxiety, Jimmie always went along with her crazy stunts, but this time Annette knew that he would never allow his wife anywhere near a live crocodile. He had seen first hand just how quickly they could gobble a native dog. At the time Brenon decided to shoot the scene, Annette claims that Jimmie just happened to have to go to New York on business for three weeks. It seems more likely that Brenon and Annette planned to have the whole thing completed in his absence. At the age of 88, when much of the past was a little blurry, Annette could still recall the scene in intricate detail:

> They were going to throw a dummy in and I said, 'No! I'll do it.' I wouldn't have a double for anything in the world. I just had that kind of a nature. Finally they brought the crocodiles in. They were the real thing. You'd take a piece of wood to them and they'd snap it in half, just like that. This is how we did the scene. The Sheik let four or five crocs through a sluice gate. It was real melodrama and they looked ferocious when they came through. But when a crocodile is lying with his mouth wide open and looks terrifying, he's actually calm. They let them all settle and they fed them well, and believe me I watched after that! I said, 'I'm ready.' I came down some steps with these eunuchs (who were the bad men who were going to throw me in). Well, just out of line with the camera there was a little ladder you could go up. The idea was one (eunuch) would take my shoulders like this . . . and then the other one my feet. And then they'd go—one, two, three plunk! and throw me in. We had to have some rehearsals. They had to make it look natural. But one of the men—I don't think he wanted to do it. He kept saying 'No for you missus, no for you!' Well, come the day, I looked at these five ferocious crocodiles and five men were out of the line of camera to one side—so that

they could go for *them* if the crocs went for *me*. But what happened was that I looked down at them [the crocs] and all of a sudden I saw one fella that looked tremendous. And I said 'Wait a minute! Wait a minute!' I said, 'Stop Herbert! Stop! I don't want to worry you but that one over there . . . I don't like the look of him. He's got a tremendous mouth and it's facing my shoulders.' I said, 'Face my feet to them, so it's not so tempting.'

As soon as she struck the water, she untied her hands 'and made for that ladder quicker than you could say "Flash".'

Two or three days later Jimmie returned from New York. Everything went along swimmingly until the film's editor came up and congratulated Annette in front of Jimmie. 'Oh Miss Kellerman, that was a wonderful take.' Jimmie immediately turned to his wife and asked her what the man was talking about. She tried to feign ignorance—unsuccessfully. Jimmie wouldn't let it go. He made the editor show him the rushes and, when he saw his wife being fed to the crocodiles, completely lost his head. Annette remembered: 'He went up to Herbert and said, "How could you let her do it?!" Then he [Brenon] said, "She was alright." I thought Jimmie was going to shoot him. They had to pull them apart.'

The tension between the two men never really dissipated. Shy, unassuming Jimmie had no time for the swaggering, posturing Brenon. 'He was just over ambitious and a spoilt man' is how Annette described him later. Nor could Brenon stand criticism, especially from someone who wasn't on the payroll. Annette was caught between the two of them. She didn't blame Brenon, taking responsibility for the risks she took with the crocodiles. 'You see that's the way I was. I'd get carried away on things. I didn't hold that against him [Brenon]. I didn't have to do it. They could have used a double.'

In the film the crocodiles were turned into white swans by a good fairy and Anitia was saved, but in reality Annette remembered it as 'one of the most horrible episodes of my life. There were many times after that that my nightmares about crocodiles were so real Jimmie had to wake me to reassure me that I was dreaming.' The irony was that no one could ever convince William Fox that the crocodiles were the real thing. After seeing the movie, he said: 'Gee those dummies are wonderful!' When Jimmie tried to tell Fox that they were real, he laughed and told him, 'Don't tell me that, tell it to the marines!'

Brenon could do without a homicidal husband on his heels; he had enough on his hands as it was. The relationship with Fox was far from the idyllic mutual admiration society it had once been. There were phone calls to and from New York and Brenon was summoned on more than one occasion. Fox had come out on location only once—before shooting started. After three months, the film was way over budget and running behind schedule. Apart from the Gnome Kingdom, Brenon had also built an entire Moorish city at a cost of $350 000. The most outstanding piece of architecture was the Sheik's palace. Not satisfied with a pasteboard exterior, Brenon had had his masons construct a fully functioning palace. He was able to shoot scenes in its exquisite interiors. He also restored a great stone fortress that had been abandoned for two centuries.

Somehow Brenon managed to keep control of the film and finish it. The *piece de resistance* was the final battle scene where the whole massive permanent structure of the city suddenly exploded into flames and was burned to the ground. Fox, whom

Annette described as 'a real Jewish business man more than anything else', must have winced when he saw $350 000 go up in smoke. It is not clear what ultimately soured the relationship between the director and the producer of A Daughter of the Gods. Years later, Annette couldn't exactly remember how the argument escalated out of all proportion, only that it came as a tremendous shock because both men had invested so much in the movie. She remembered Fox telling Herbert he spent too much.

One problem may have been with Brenon's mother. She was a very wealthy woman, and Herbert didn't really have to work. He consulted her on every aspect of the film. The fact that he was a mummy's boy, and Fox was a Hungarian immigrant who had built his career from scratch, may have been the source of their mutual attraction in the first place, but it was also what finally caused the ructions between the two men. Annette recalled:

> Herbert Brenon's worst enemy was his mother. She was one of those mothers. She went everywhere with him and everything that Herbert did was just right. Whether she egged him on to this and that I don't know. All of a sudden they [Brenon and Fox] were fighting like cat and dog.

Annette also believed that the scope of the film (the first million dollar budget) also strained their relationship. One bamboozled journalist tried to conceive of the reality of a million of anything:

> What does 1 000 000 or a million really mean to you? It is utterly impossible for the average person to conceive of a million dollars, bushels, miles or things. Astronomers and geologists who habitually deal in large numbers, say that it is

next to impossible to visualise a million—to them a small number. Standing shoulder to shoulder 1 000 000 people would make a solid wall of humanity from New York to Syracuse—a distance of 290 miles. These comparisons may serve to give at least a faint idea of what it means to say that $1 million was spent by William Fox in the making of one picture—the first time it has ever been done in the motion picture industry.

Whatever the dispute was about, it is certain that Fox fired Brenon before the film was even cut. On the boat back to New York, after they had finished the picture, Annette and Brenon also had a disagreement. 'The way he spoke to me!' she said. 'We were just a few hours out from New York. Herbert said, "Well, as far as I'm concerned you're not going to do anymore pictures."' Annette was shocked—she loved working with Brenon. They collaborated closely and, like Jimmie and her father, Brenon was the male collaborator Annette needed to release her creativity. In Herbert Brenon's case, the relationship was in many ways more intense because the scale and expectations involved in making the film meant they had to spend most of their time together. Though there is no question that there was a physical relationship between the two, there definitely was a strong attraction. 'I was always the first to admit that Herbert Brenon was very good for me,' Annette said later. Jimmie was quiet and reliable but Brenon was her match in energy and daring. He was charming, articulate, eccentric and autocratic— everyone he met fell under his spell. When she was 88, Annette was still incredulous that, after the argument, she never saw him, let alone worked with him, again. She wasn't just disappointed or sad, she told Joel Greenberg: 'I was really heartbroken.' The attraction wasn't just one-sided. Brenon told a reporter from the *Cincinnati Herald*:

> When I go to the theatre to see Annette Kellerman's act, I want to sit in the back and imagine her a wonderful, animated bronze, rather than a human being. There was never a figure more inspiring to artist or sculptor than Miss Kellerman's when she is poised on the tip of a spring-board just before she leaps into the air. The ancient Greek masterpieces look gross beside her.

Annette had seen a future with Brenon, making the motion pictures she liked in the way she wanted. She went on to make other movies, but she lost her enthusiasm after *A Daughter of the Gods*. 'He never did anything again, you know,' she said later of Brenon's post *Daughter of the Gods* career. This was clearly sour grapes on Annette's part, as Brenon did in fact go on to become arguably one of the top two or three directors in the 1920s in terms of box office clout. He really had very few rivals in those days, apart from perhaps De Mille, making some big budget movies including *Beau Geste* with Ronald Coleman as well as *Peter Pan*. Critics spoke with admiration of 'the Brenon Touch'. Brenon was not invited to attend the opening night of *A Daughter of the Gods*, as William Fox had banned him from all theatres where the film was being shown. That didn't dissuade him though; he was spotted at the premiere in the second row in hand-me-down clothes and a crepe hair Van Dyke beard. While Brenon fought for his rightful credits in court, his name was removed from the film and replaced with his enemy's—Fox had declared himself director, producer and author. It was finally resolved after several months and the newspapers were again citing Herbert Brenon as the author and director.

When the film opened at the Lyric Theatre in New York on 19 October 1916, no one knew about the dispute between the leading lady, the producer and the director. *A Daughter of the Gods* was in every way more sophisticated than *Neptune's Daughter*. In the two years since the release of Annette's first film, publicity had also become increasingly sophisticated. There were ads in the industry papers explaining to cinema owners just how the Fox Corporation wanted to market the film. Each cinema was given paper tape measures to hand out to the ladies in the audience and a cardboard cutout of Annette Kellerman was placed in the foyer. Annette's measurements were also prominently displayed. Women were given the opportunity to compare their own vital statistics with those of the Perfect Woman. There were also art competitions for those who could paint the best reproduction of this effigy of the star. Fox Corporation ads advised cinema owners that ticket prices were to range from 25c to $1 depending on the clientele:

> The wise manager will not overlook the great advertising opportunities in connection with *A Daughter of the Gods* and Annette Kellerman. It is a chance to delight the public and at the same time realise unusual profits.

Pre-publicity was also much more in evidence than with *Neptune's Daughter* in the lead-up to the film's release. The public learned that *A Daughter of the* Gods would afford them many further glimpses of Annette's famous figure. Fox had to tread a fine line between the obvious titillation of the movie's biggest, often naked asset, Annette, and the morals of the audience they were wishing to attract. The same double standard applied in movies as it had in vaudeville. The middle class was coaxed into believing that the motive for Annette's near-nakedness was artistic rather than sexual. A publicity shot of Annette sitting almost nude on a rock below a waterfall was declared by the *Atlanta Constitution* to be: 'One of the most artistic creations of the camera. Many of the most prominent artists in the United States . . . claim that the posture, together with the lighting, is most wonderful.'

Professor Carl Sloertzer of Leipzig, Germany, who had spent months photographing birds in Central America and in the mountains of Panama, was shown the still of Annette and 'pronounced it to be the best he's ever seen, particularly as to pose and lighting'. The photographic expert Lieutenant Carl Swenson of the Swedish Navy, who had just returned from unearthing 'an early Incan Temple and untold treasure', also admired the photo. 'Lieutenant Swenson, while refusing to discuss the treasure, praises the photo most kindly and declared it was one of the most artistic he had seen.' The article gave readers a wet sarong photo of Annette as a sample of what was to come when the movie was released, but the two expert opinions made the forthcoming vision of Annette in *A Daughter of the Gods* seem artistic and even educational. When the film was released most reviewers fell into line. There were:

> many scenes in which Miss Kellerman and many other girls appear in the nude. Yet no one can have the least grounds to complain regarding this, because this part of the offering has been delightfully handled, and there is no more reason to have a suggestive thought in viewing this offering than there would be in viewing sculpture to be found in any of our great art collections.

A few maverick reviewers didn't take the Greek statue analogy quite so seriously, however:

Annette Kellerman . . . while she hasn't enough clothes on to flag a handcar, proved a magnet that drew a capacity audience . . . Clothes may make the man but they don't make a daughter of the gods, at least not the sort Annette depicts. And watching her disport herself *a la Phryne*, [who was a Greek courtesan not a statue] one must realise that, as a matter of form, the photoplay is a success . . . Anitia, after wandering round like the sewing machine that doesn't have a stitch on, is captured and taken to the Sultan's Harem.

Another critic wrote: 'Aubrey Munson [another star who wore little clothing] has nothing on Annette Kellerman, and as it has elsewhere been observed, neither has Miss Kellerman.'

Ironically, Annette later denied that she was actually nude, claiming 'I had a very thin pair of tights on.' In the stills that remain, however, whatever she was wearing, if anything, is not in evidence. Certainly John Watson wasn't going back to see *A Daughter of the Gods* over and over again because he believed Annette was wearing tights. According to the *Toledo Blade,* he presented:

a pitiful sight when he appeared in police court as a witness against his wife, whom he accused of having assaulted him . . . bandages covered four deep gashes in his head, inflicted, he told the mayor, by a potato masher in the hands of his wife. Mrs Watson pleaded not guilty to the charge. 'You see,' she explained to the mayor, 'I assaulted him alright but I contend that I had a right to do it. That scoundrel,' she said, shaking her fist at her husband, 'went to see that Annette Kellerman movie three times in three days and he'd tell me every night what a pretty form she had.

The film was not judged solely on the merits of Annette's body. Her stunts were amazing then, and even by today's standards they were very daring. More than one critic was converted to giving women the vote when they saw her perform. The *New York Times Journal* said:

Those who contend that woman is too weak physically to contend with a man at the voting booth and therefore should be denied the franchise, should go to see Annette Kellerman in *Daughter of the Gods*.

The *Boston Post* concurred:

She displays a courage that is nothing short of divine. After seeing her one may feel like defying any ten foot man in the audience to declare that the sex of which she is an ideal example hasn't the courage to fight or the ability to vote or do anything else they choose to do. If votes were obtained by physical or mental courage, Miss Kellerman would demand a million of them.

The film employed new techniques which had never been seen before. Brenon used a method of tinting that looked almost like natural colour. The editing, too, was much quicker and more dramatic than ever before. This impressed the *New York Dramtic News*:

With almost kaleidoscopic swiftness scenes pile upon one another, fall for a moment all too brief on the screen, and are gone. A distinct advantage would appear to have been made in motion picture production. The actual mechanical perfection of the film has probably never been equalled. Camera effects, dissolves and unique photographic feats abound.

Undoubtedly, 1916 was the year of the epic film. Only a couple of months before *A Daughter of the Gods,* D.W. Griffiths had released *Birth of a Nation.* Both films ran for well over three hours. The latter survived, but *A Daughter of the Gods* was lost. It is not known how this happened, but it was the fate of many early movies—film stock was made of nitrate which was highly flammable and prone to self-combustion. The films were not necessarily made to last. Because of the rapid advances in technology, films were often totally outmoded a year after their release. Moviemakers reused old film stock and filmed over it. Any one of these things could have happened to *A Daughter of the Gods.*

'Its loss is tragic. Not only was *A Daughter of the Gods* an eye-popping spectacle and a wildly imaginative fantasy,' writes film historian Frank Thompson, '[but] it might also have been one of the masterpieces of the silent cinema.' Publicity, reviews and stills are all that survive of the film. These show the incredible sets and battle scenes with 20 000 extras. Publicity shots from newspapers of the day have intriguing captions with plenty of capital letters for breathtaking emphasis. Annette, reclining on a chaise longue, is 'Surrounded by Her Slaves and Handmaidens. She lives in Opulent Luxury.' The detail of the set is astounding. A live peacock stands in the foreground as exotically clad women languorously disport themselves. Nubian slaves fan them, proffering sherbets while another peacock trails its long feathers across the dazzling marble floor. There is a shot that reveals Annette, in a harem outfit, raising her arms above what looks like a stuffed peacock with the caption, 'The Daughter of the Gods Dances in Weird Measure.'

Amongst other tantalising glimpses of this lost film are stills of a 20 000 strong army crossing a huge desert towards

the Moorish city, and thousands of soldiers clashing swords and
shields in a battle scene on the giant steps of the temple.

W. Stephen Bush of *Motion Picture News* compared the film
favourably to Griffith's masterpiece of the day:

> It has a touch of *The Birth of a Nation* but not one of these
> touches was plagiaristic . . . this magnificent production has
> great merit on its own not to be found in any part of our screen
> literature . . . and greater than this—the irresistible eternal
> feminine.

According to the *Louisville Herald*, nothing like this film had
ever before been 'exhibited in the history of cinema and there
is small possibility of this tribute to art ever being duplicated'.
It is difficult to say exactly how an audience would view the film
today, as silent films had their own rhythm and convention.
They were more stately but could move quickly when the story
required. There was a standard long shot, medium shot and
close-up technique to most films of the time, though silent film
expert Frank Thompson believes that, in 'a film like *Daughter of
the Gods* they would probably have lingered a little longer just to
let your eye fill with all the detail on the screen'.

Annette always regretted that she had never kept a copy of
her films. 'I don't have anything at all,' she said in old age, 'I'm
terribly sorry. I was very careless. I've got a few stills.'

What is known is that, though the film was presented as a
simple fairytale, the storyline—like the tales from the *Thousand
and One Nights* which inspired it—was very convoluted. It involved
two birds who die but are reincarnated—one as the son of a
cruel Sultan and the other as Anitia, 'a creature born of sunlight
and sea'. At the beginning of the film, audiences were asked to

forget about being adults and, for one night: 'Let us return to our mother's knees tonight, with fairies and witches and gnomes and elves and be as little children to enter a heaven of rich enjoyment.' In reality, *A Daughter of the Gods* was closer to the epic saga of the *Ring Cycle*. In fact, W. Stephen Bush, praising the film's musical accompaniment by Robert Hood Bowers, wrote that 'here and there I recognized a Wagnerian motif handled with uncommon skill'. *Photoplay's* Julian Johnson called it 'as grand a tale of nereids and necromancy . . . as was ever wrought outside the Burton edition of *The Thousand and One Nights*'.

Not everyone was convinced by the story. The reviewer from the *Boston Transcript* wrote:

> Considered as a play or a plot or an idea or a lesson, moral or immoral or unmortal, *Daughter of the Gods* is drivel. It is worse than that, it is such a meaningless hodge podge of pseudo-allegorical absurdities as might be developed in a nightmare or conceived in a madhouse.

But even this critic couldn't resist the film as a spectacle, going on to say: 'in the way of rushing, gesticulating, fighting galloping crowds—it is magnificent. The whole thing is worthwhile to see.'

Annette was now one of the most famous women of the day. Her films were shown not only in America, but throughout Europe. The segments from *Neptune's Daughter* discovered in the Museum of Modern Art in New York reveal that she was popular as far away as Russia; the film is subtitled in that language. She criss-crossed the nation, attending opening nights and speaking afterwards to adoring fans. At the Washington premiere, President Woodrow Wilson and his wife were in the audience. The *Chicago Herald* reported:

Both the president and Mrs Wilson have seen motion pictures before, but never in a theatre. Hitherto they have seen photoplays at the White House or at private entertainments. The President was greatly pleased with the picture and said that *A Daughter of the Gods* was a wonderful film.

At another opening, Annette attended, and the *Pittsburgh Leader* reported:

> she was lead [*sic*] out in front of the blue plush curtains and showered with flowers of every description . . . Miss Kellerman was two thirds of the show whether she was on the screen or in real flesh and blood, bowing and smiling to one of the biggest audiences Pittsburgh has ever seen.

There were endless articles about what Annette thought, what she wore and what she ate. Fox wanted her to sign a five-picture deal, but Annette decided to take it one picture at a time. She made only one more movie for Fox, *Queen of the Sea,* yet again thinking nothing of risking her life in the pursuit of bigger and more breathtaking stunts.

11
THE MOST DRAMATIC EPISODE OF MY LIFE

Headlining in Pittsburgh in 1916, Annette was waiting in the wings one night to make her entrance when she became absorbed by the act on stage. She saw a rather fleshy man dancing nimbly about on a tiny wire, strung high above the audience who watched, holding its breath. 'Who's that?' Annette asked a stagehand who was equally entranced 'Who's that? Only Birdie Millman, the famous wirewalker, that's all,' he told her. She was spellbound, and wrote in 'My Story' that she decided then and there: 'I'm going to do that. Diving's given me a good sense of balance. There's no reason why I shouldn't become quite an expert at wire walking.'

After the excitement of *A Daughter of the Gods*, she craved something new and different for her vaudeville act. She remembered her friends The Dunedins, a tightrope-walking and fancy-cycling duo from New Zealand, and asked them whether they could teach her and help her with her first wire-walking rig. They thought she was crazy, and told her it took years to master their art. This, of course, only made Annette more determined.

From that moment on, every morning she could be found in the semi-darkened theatre practising her wire dance, surrounded by all the other performers in rehearsal—acrobats, jugglers, unicyclists, dancers and animal acts. Annette loved starting the day with a challenge, honing the improbable skill that not a soul believed she would ever master—except, of course, Jimmie. He would often sit backstage, chatting to the different performers or playing the piano in the orchestra pit, quietly proud of his ever-ambitious wife, walking above him with a parasol in her hands and a determined smile on her face.

By the time William Fox saw her dancing on a wire way above the stage, she had mastered the art. He was so impressed he wanted her to come up with a new diving stunt which included her latest skill for their next project, *Queen of the Sea*.

The character Annette was to play was required to escape yet again from a tower, but this time, instead of just diving, she was to tightrope walk high above a raging sea. Between her shows at the Hippodrome, where she was performing her huge *Mermaid Spectacular*, she practised this stunt for six months. A 100 foot rope was slung across the stage from both wings. The length meant that the rope was more likely to dip and sway; after the short tight wires she had learnt on, she had to adapt to the extra movement of the slack.

When it came to shooting the scene in Bar Harbor in Maine, the wire strung between two old lighthouses had an even longer span of 150 feet and, despite a dozen guy ropes and weights, could not be kept anywhere near taut enough. The day was windy and getting more so by the minute:

> I was 60–70 feet up. I was a good wire walker because I'd been doing it on stage. But it's a different proposition getting way

up there. And for 14 feet I had to walk over rocks and that 14 feet seemed about a thousand. It swayed, I had pains in my calves and my legs trying to control that wire.

The distance seemed so long because Annette had to walk over shallow water with sharp rocks only 3 feet below the surface—one small mistake would see her landing right on top of them. It took her three weeks to work up the courage to do it, but when she did the whole of Bar Harbor high society was there to watch her. The *New York Telegraph* reported:

> She practised and waited days for a favourable wind until the waiting got on her nerves and she finally announced she was going to walk the next day and, true to her word, she did, although almost blown from the top of the tower to which the wire was anchored. In her dive the gale turned her in the air but she straightened out her body and struck the water perfectly.

Annette had the assistance of the United States Navy for her stunt. There were also plenty of ships coming to Bar Harbor when they heard Annette Kellerman was down there. As she prepared to dive, the Navy patrolled the waters below making sure none of those vessels came into shot.

From the beginning, Annette didn't feel good about doing the picture. Firstly, she was working with a new team. 'I didn't have Herbert,' she said later. 'And John Adolfi wasn't much of a director.' Annette simply didn't have the same spark with Adolfi as with Brenon, but he can't have been as inept as she remembered. He made many big-budget silent films before successfully moving over to the talkies and directing both Bette Davis and James Cagney in the early 1930s. The fact that the film was not shot in exotic Jamiaca or Bermuda, but plain old Bar Harbor, may also have been a let down for the adventurous Annette. What really cast a pall over the project, even before shooting started, was the accident she had while training for the extensive riding scenes in the film—'the most dramatic episode in my life,' she called it in 'My Story'.

Annette would ride every day across the moors at Montauk Point at the east end of Long Island. She had brought her own horse, but the stable which sold it to her 'forgot to tell me that, though the horse was a good one, it had a habit of bucking. One day while I was out riding, the horse decided to have its own buck jumping contest but failed to give me any warning.' She was thrown from the horse into a puddle which hid a large rock, which struck her spine and she immediately lost consciousness. Meanwhile, Jimmie was back at the Montauk Inn becoming increasingly uneasy about Annette. She had been away much longer than usual. The guests tried to reassure him until one of them noticed a white spot in the distance. Jimmie went to the window and gasped 'She wears a white riding suit!' He jumped into a car and found his wife in the puddle of mud and water, dirty and unconscious. The nearest doctor travelled from 14 miles away, and by the time he arrived Jimmie was in a bad state. He was just a local doctor and his only advice was that Annette not be moved. The next day Jimmie called a specialist. The two doctors consulted and decided that nothing could be done until the swelling on her back subsided and they could ascertain whether the spine was broken. Annette was in shock. She refused to eat and drink and lay in the bed slightly delirious, staring at the ceiling. She wrote about the incident in 'My Story':

Some marking on it looked like the foot of Italy and I kept repeating 'It looks just like a foot, a boot.' Then I began to think about the future. 'I'll never be able to swim again. I can't move my legs. Oh I don't want to lie here for the rest of my life!'

Though she was feeling very low, she could see that her husband was suffering too. 'Poor Jimmie! Every time he came in, I could tell he'd been crying. Don't tell me men don't cry.'

At last the doctors were able to examine her spine. They sat her up on the edge of the bed and she immediately fainted. Later she came to and Jimmie was there. She knew by the look on his face that the doctors had told him she'd never walk again. This was exactly what Annette needed to shake herself out of self-pity. After all, hadn't she overcome being crippled, learned to walk without braces and become a champion? She made the decision there and then she would walk once more.

First, Annette had to see whether she could actually move her feet. She concentrated and, though it was agony, felt them move a fraction. She decided she'd only fainted because she hadn't eaten for two days. She called the nurse, who came expecting to see a poor sad girl who was starving herself to death because she didn't want to live. Annette ordered her to: 'Go down and get me something to eat. I want some soup and some chicken. Go on, bring me lots of food. It's about time I ate something.' The nurse thought the patient was delirious, but decided to humour her and brought the food. When she had made herself eat it all, Annette told the nurse to come back and bring a watch. 'AND DON'T TELL MR SULLIVAN about any of this.'

When the nurse returned, Annette made her help her to the edge of the bed, then sit her up. She says in 'My Story': 'The agony was awful but I didn't let her know. I managed to whisper:

"Watch the time and tell me when three minutes are up." I fought against fainting and stuck it out . . . at the end I was still conscious.' The poor nurse was then persuaded to flout all her knowledge about spinal injuries and to help the patient to stand. Though the pain was intense, Annette walked across the room and back to the bed. When Annette finally told the nurse to bring her robe because she was going to walk to her husband downstairs, the bewildered woman offered no resistance. She wrote:

> It took me a long time to get down the hall. Little by little I arrived at the head of the wide, old-fashioned staircase that led down to the big living room of the Inn. This was the scene that met my eyes. In the corner of the room Jimmie was sitting on one of those wall seats and all about him were the guests of the Inn. They were all trying to tell him that the doctors' decision was not a final one. Suddenly he looked up and saw me—he thought he was seeing a ghost. He rushed towards me coming fast up the stairs calling, 'Sweet! Sweet!' I was so anxious to get down alone that all I said was 'No, let me do it by myself.' There were only nine or ten steps but it seemed like many miles. When I got to the bottom I almost fell but was caught by Jimmie. That effort kept me flat on my back for some time.

The film was put on hold indefinitely. The doctors had told Jimmie that his wife would never swim again and that dancing would also be a thing of the past. For the first time in her life, she had to rely totally on her husband. Every morning he was there helping her out of bed and taking her over to the *barre* so she could do her ballet routine. When she first started she was only able to lift her leg 6 inches off the ground and swimming was out of the question because the cold water hurt her spine.

But, like any true heroine, Annette recovered—though very slowly. After a year of following a physiotherapy regime of her own devising, she was able to swim and dive again. She was ready to do her famous stunt from the tower in Bar Harbor.

The residents of the exclusive summer colony at Bar Harbor were very pleased to have mermaids on their beaches. The *New York Telegraph* reported: 'Watching the making of *Queen of the Seas* became society's diversion and thousands visited the "locations" at Sun Rocks or at Sand Beach.' As one journalist put it, 'Millionaires whose wealth is said to aggregate $400 000 000 witnessed the photographing.' And great things were expected of the film by theatre managers. The *Exhibitor's Bulletin,* an industry magazine, didn't beat about the bush, promising not artistic shots or Greek statues, but instead:

> As a breath of salt air stirs the torpid blood so will *Queen of the Sea* affect your box office . . . The trickle of wandering waters will echo in your till like the tinkle of spilt coin. *Queen of the Sea* will mean the only touch of vacation to enter the lives of thousands who patronize your theatre . . . They will discover Annette Kellerman, while a Diving Venus, is not a Lady Godiva; and her shapely entourage are not so stingy as that dame when it comes to a showdown. You won't strain your eyes trying to follow the flitting forms of these darting divinities of the deep. You get more than a flash—much more. This is the naked truth.

Along with nakedness, the film promised a scene where Annette would be chained in a dungeon and attacked by live ferrets, a life and death battle in the boiling surf, an escape from death by revolving knives and a fall from the clouds into the yawning ocean. Despite its promise, the picture was not as well received as *A Daughter of the Gods*. Though publicity claimed that 'the film will be entirely different in action and in story to *Daughter of the Gods*', and that it was 'greater than *Daughter of the Gods*, greater in fact than any other screen story that has ever been attempted', *Queen of the Sea* was virtually just a rehash, and not a very imaginative one, with the 'Daughter' being promoted to 'Queen'.

In the two years since the release of *A Daughter of the Gods*, America had joined the war against the Kaiser and times had changed. It seemed that tales of real people, not mermaids, were what the public wanted to see.

Annette's next film, *What Women Love,* was a departure from her earlier pictures. Moving with the times, Annette was cast as a modern-day heroine, Annabel Cotton. This time she donned boxing gloves instead of a mermaid's tail, and the film was a comedy rather than a fairy story. With her hair cut in a fashionable bob, Annette, as Annabel, 'came up to all expectations, and naturally, she is in the thickest of everything from swimming and diving to fighting foes that would do her physical harm'. The same reviewer also praised her dramatic abilities. For this picture Annette did another stint in the rapids and there were plenty of fights where the plucky Annabel stood up for herself on land and underwater. As Annette put it, 'I was playing one of those women who wanted to get out and do something all the time.'

Annabel is a 'lively young miss who loves to gambol upon the beach sands and green lawns in the attire best suited for water antics'. She is set upon by women from the town's Purity League, who try unsuccessfully to reform her. She is also the wife of a 'namby-pamby' husband who happens to own a beautiful yacht, giving Annette the opportunity for a new and dangerous stunt. 'I had to dive from the mast and I only cleared the boat by that much,' she told Joel Greenberg, holding her hands a few inches apart. 'Jimmie couldn't believe I didn't get hurt.' In fact, Jimmie begged Annette to substitute a dummy for her in this stunt—he was never the same after the crocodile incident. So he had a figure made up, dressed it in one of Annette's bathing suits and hauled it up the mast. Mipps, who was an eyewitness, describes what happened next in her memoirs:

> Pouf! off she went, whirling and twirling around in the breeze. First one arm was gone with the wind and then followed a leg the same way and the remains floated down on the water and sank (and so did we . . . in hysterics). Annette promptly got up and said, 'Are you satisfied now? *I'll* do it.' She was up that mast and out to the edge in a beautiful dive, away and safe from the intruding baddie.

Annette enjoyed making this film because, for the first time since Herbert Brenon, she really admired the director. Lois Weber had begun her film career as an actress, often starring alongside her husband, Phillip Smalley. By 1913 Weber was directing films and by 1916, working at Universal, she was one of the highest-paid directors in the world. In 1917 Weber formed her own production company and her career flourished until the early 1920s. One of the most energetic, aesthetically ambitious and technically well-grounded film-makers in the industry, she wrote, produced and directed social dramas with modern themes. These dealt with issues like birth control, abortion and inter-generational conflict. It seems strange that she was given a light fluffy comedy like *What Women Love* to direct, but perhaps she wanted to work with Annette who was also by this time an exemplar of the modern woman. She had revolutionised women's fashion and was still causing a stir in downtown Los Angeles when she went shopping in trousers. Unfortunately, Lois was replaced. Nate Watt, who took over, can't have been quite as inspiring. Although he assisted on some classic films of the 1930s, including *All Quiet on the Western Front* and *Of Mice and Men*, his claim to fame as a director in his own right was the *Hopalong Cassidy* series in the 1930s. He ended his career in 1961 on a particularly low note with a B picture called *Fiend of Dope Island*. Independent Producer Sol Lesser put $600 000 into *What Women Love* and was repaid with moderate success, though nothing like that achieved by *A Daughter of the Gods*.

Annette made only one more movie after this, a low-budget feature shot in New Zealand titled *Venus of the South Seas*. Though fragments of *Neptune's Daughter* have survived, *Venus* is the only complete film featuring Annette in existence—a nitrate print of it was discovered in a London basement in the early 1980s. As Annette herself admitted, it was far from her best film. 'That wasn't good at all. I was out in New Zealand and somebody came up and asked Jimmie if we'd do a picture. So I said yes. I was not so young anymore.' She was 36 years old in 1922 when the film was made. She looks terrific but the story, though it had all the elements of her other films—plenty of scenes where she swims, dives and fights underwater—is lacklustre and old-fashioned. According to the *1924 Modern Picture Booking Guide*, Annette plays:

> A girl raised on a lonely isle who meets and falls in love with
> a wealthy young man. He goes away, but decides to return.
> When her father, a pearl diver, dies, she sets out for civilization,
> but meets with obstacles, which the return of her lover solves.

The film is interesting only insofar as it gives an idea of Annette's screen appeal. Despite manifesting many of the stilted gestures of the silent film era, she manages to appear remarkably natural on screen. The most fascinating insight comes from the fairytale sequence where Annette plays a mermaid at home beneath the sea. Smiling at herself in the mirror as she carefully applies her lipstick and fixes her hair, she is simply beautiful. Though natural enough on land, underwater she really comes to life—turning somersaults and gliding through the water as naturally and as gracefully as any mermaid. The scene gives a glimpse of why audiences flocked to see both her stage shows and her films. Perhaps one of the reasons that Annette appears so relaxed is that Jimmie was directing.

It was in New Zealand that Jimmie became really interested in underwater photography, and it was there that he had a chance to use some of the latest equipment. Annette had been in New Zealand doing a vaudeville tour in 1922 when a Christchurch syndicate, New Zealand Dominion Productions, approached her offering a starring role in a film they were to produce. She accepted and Jimmie agreed to direct. He decided to shoot the interiors in Christchurch and moved to Nelson to film the exteriors and underwater sequences. Even though the $10 000 budget was small compared with those for her earlier films, a Hollywood film crew and equipment were brought out and filming began in August 1922. Back in America, the footage was edited and titled, and the film was released and distributed in New Zealand in April 1924. Expecting to see a film that promoted Nelson and New Zealand, local investors were to be sadly disappointed. New Zealand was never mentioned, much less Nelson, with the publicity describing the film as having been made in the South Sea Islands. But Annette had had enough of films by then and was ready to go back to her true love, one she'd never really abandoned—vaudeville.

12

GIVE ME THE WIDE OPEN SPACES

When Fox offered Annette a five-picture deal after *A Daughter of the Gods*, she was horrified by the idea, though it was the kind of offer other big stars of the day would have jumped at. 'To sit in the audience and watch yourself on the screen is a poor substitute to anyone who has been on the other side of the footlights,' she wrote in *How to Swim*. Jimmie thought it could be a good career move, but Annette wasn't sure. 'Listen, Jimmie, you and I are nomads,' she argued. 'We love the theatre. Picture work is grand but give me the wide open spaces—free to go when and where we like.'

It seems a strange decision in retrospect, to quit movies just when they were taking off and go back to vaudeville, which, in America at least, was in its death throes. The vaudeville theatres Annette had performed in the season before were rapidly being transformed into movie palaces. There were some very good reasons why Annette should want out of the picture industry. At the time mermaid movies were all very well, but as motion pictures became more sophisticated, so did their audiences. They didn't want to see an imaginary fairyland, but modern dramas and comedy, which was why *What Women Love* did so well. It must be remembered too that, by the time Annette made her last film, *Venus of the South Seas,* the talkies were about to begin. The type of movies she had been making—convoluted stories with dramatic stunts set in lavish locations—were the first to go, because the logistics of recording dialogue meant that they had to be made in studios. Sound was the star of the early talkies— in one of the very first talking pictures, the audience broke into spontaneous applause when they saw some bacon cooking on a stove and *heard* it spitting and crackling. Annette also realised how difficult it would have been for the public to accept her as anything other than an action heroine who dived and swam in every picture. She said later that if she'd stayed in the movies she 'would have ended up as a Tarzan, that's all, going from tree to tree'.

Perhaps the strongest reason of all for leaving motion pictures was that theatre was her first and abiding love. She missed the immediacy of its audience and the fact that things could go wrong. When she stumbled and fell running up to perform a dive, she laughed at the hole in her stocking, hobbled up again, made the dive, bowed and limped off stage to thunderous applause.

While most vaudevillians travelled by train on tour, Annette loved to drive around the country in her white Buick. The constant movement kept her going—it was her life's blood. The physical realities of transporting her huge tank across the length and breadth of the country were left to Jimmie. Ten feet deep and containing more than 10 000 gallons, the tank arrived in sections. The 'bumping in' and 'striking' at each venue were particularly elaborate. The specialised technician who accompanied every tour had to assemble the tank in an oval

A still from *Queen of the Sea*, Annette's third Hollywood film. (Courtesy Hilton Cordell Productions)

Annette always claimed she wore a body stocking in her films, though photographs like this one, from *A Daughter of the Gods*, tell a different story. (Courtesy Hilton Cordell Productions)

Left: Annette performed all her own stunts—including diving from a lighthouse at New York's chic Bar Harbor for *Queen of the Sea*. Watching the filming from the shore became the thing to do amongst the well-heeled locals. (Courtesy Barbara Firth) **Right**: A scene from *Queen of the Sea*, with Annette in suitably melodramatic silent-film mode. (Courtesy Barbara Firth)

The cast of one of Annette's European vaudeville shows, shown here in Rotterdam in 1931. Annette can be seen in the back row, fourth from the right. (Mitchell Library SLNSW)

Annette wows the crowds on a French beach, during her eight-year European vaudeville tour. (Mitchell Library SLNSW)

Two stills from underwater footage taken by Jimmie at Silver Springs, Florida. Both display Annette's grace and athleticism under the water, but only the photo at right, with Annette's face showing, gives some clue to her age—she was 51 years old at the time. (Mitchell Library SLNSW)

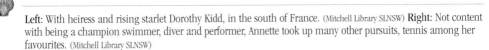

Left: With heiress and rising starlet Dorothy Kidd, in the south of France. (Mitchell Library SLNSW) **Right:** Not content with being a champion swimmer, diver and performer, Annette took up many other pursuits, tennis among her favourites. (Mitchell Library SLNSW)

Annette counted Grace Kelly (right), whose wedding shower she attended, among her friends. (Courtesy Barbara Firth)

Left: A glamorous Annette as she appeared on the cover of a Dutch magazine advertising her stage appearances in that country. (Mitchell Library SLNSW) **Right:** A signed photograph from another close friend, Lucille Ball. (Mitchell Library SLNSW)

The ageing star with Esther Williams, who played Annette in *The Million Dollar Mermaid*, the 1952 Hollywood film of Annette's life. (Courtesy Barbara Firth)

Annette and friend outside Annette's Californian health food shop, which opened in the early 1950s. (Mitchell Library SLNSW)

Annette and Jimmie enjoyed a loving and respectful marriage for 60 years. (Courtesy Hilton Cordell Productions)

Left: Well into her seventies, Annette still displayed astonishing flexibility and physical poise. (Courtesy Barbara Firth)
Right: Annette, photographed by Jimmie, by the pool at the Gold Coast's Chevron Hotel, where she swam daily in her old age. (Courtesy Barbara Firth)

Annette and Jimmy celebrate both Annette's birthday and America's Independence Day in Australia.
(Courtesy Barbara Firth)

Surf lifesavers carry Annette's coffin at her Gold Coast funeral, November 1975. (Courtesy Barbara Firth)

Southport Surf Club members acting as pall bearers at the funeral of Annette Kellerman. The picture also shows some of the people in the guard of honour.

80 in last tribute to the 'Million Dollar Mermaid'

A quiet farewell
for Annette

THE Gold Coast yes-
terday said a quiet
but reverent farewell
to one of its most

of the aisle.
    Six pall bearen
the Southport Sur
and Legacy carrie
Kellerman's coffin,

shape, rather like a cooper putting together a cask. When it was all in one piece, the stage had to be sawn out, known in showbiz as 'making a trap', so the tank could lie flush with the stage floor. Prior to each performance the tank was filled with water that had to be heated to exactly 72 degrees Fahrenheit, so, according to the *Rochester Post* 'the little Australian Lady doesn't suffer from the cold while entertaining her audiences'. Before the show could move on to the next theatre, the tank had to be dismantled and the stage restored to its original state.

While her films made her famous all over the world, Annette always remembered that it was on the stage that she had really achieved her fame. In 1912, three years before the release of *Neptune's Daughter*, she was already performing with one of theatre's most famous theatrical stars, Al Jolson, in a musical called *Vera Violetta*. Annette also broke all Boston box office records despite being up against the legendary Scottish music hall entertainer, Harry Lauder. The tank that had made her famous was becoming a millstone around her neck. She was reported in one newspaper as saying:

> I have spent thousands of dollars on my voice and my dancing. I have studied dramatic art and slaved to fit myself for straight acting—and I can't even get a chance to show them. I wouldn't mind doing dives and rescues in a play where there's a plot. But this eternal tank has got on my nerves. There's no future to it. I can't go jumping off springboards all my life and climbing up pasteboard rocks and jumping off again.

In 1915, after her return from Paris, Annette at last had the opportunity to star in a musical comedy written especially for and around her particular talents. In *The Model Girl*, she was given the opportunity to show off her dancing, even use the singing talent she had developed during her time in France. *Cincinnati Everyman* reported:

> She also attempts to sing but in a very modest and discreet manner. She has several opportunities to act, that is to speak lines, and this she does in a very acceptable way . . . but . . . while she discharges her duties in a very clever manner, that alone does not make the show.

It seems that the storyline was all over the place and the songs were not overwhelmingly catchy. It must have been difficult for Annette after the rave reviews for *Neptune's Daughter* to read the critic from the *Cincinatti Everyman*: 'There is little to say for the *Model Girl* as a musical comedy, it is more or less hopeless.'

Luckily not everybody agreed. *The Model Girl* was moderately successful and even toured simply on the merits of its star. The *Toledo Blade* said:

> She was found to possess art, beauty and grace exceeding the claims of advance publicity. She possesses considerable histrionic ability and can sing, though she probably will never gain access to the prima donna class.

Annette believed at last she had established herself on the dramatic stage. However, this was not really the case because, although she would act and dance on the American vaudeville circuit for another four years, she would never appear without a display of diving and swimming. Only once was she free from the tank, and that was not on the vaudeville circuit but in the heady atmosphere of the Metropolitan Opera House. She was asked to appear at a huge benefit night there by Daniel Frohman, the famous theatrical manager and producer. It was 1917, America had just entered the war and Frohman was organising a benefit for the War Fund.

In 'My Story', Annette wrote 'Needless to say this was this biggest thrill of my whole career—to dance at the Metropolitan Opera House with a ninety piece orchestra.' Even more exciting still, the orchestra was conducted by Arturo Toscanini. Representing the film world, Annette would be performing on a dream bill that was to include the most celebrated opera singers of the day—Geraldine Farrar, Antonio Scotti and Caruso singing from *Madame Butterfly*, Fritz Kreizler the world-famous violinist and Nazimova, one of the most popular theatrical actresses in America. She was overjoyed to be without a tank, a diving board or a bathing suit. Covered in sequins and feathers, she gave an impersonation of Pavlova in Saint Saen's *Swan*. 'Her beloved dancing,' wrote Mipps in 'Let's Do Something', 'had at last been recognised *and* at the Metropolitan. It gave her more satisfaction than any other performance she'd given ever.'

For over a year and a half, Annette had been spending up to six hours a day at Signor Luigi Albertieri's Dancing Academy and, amazingly, she had succeeded in becoming a proficient ballerina. The *New York Star* wrote on 16 May 1917: 'Signor Luigi Albertieri is the recipient of many congratulations on the surprise he helped Miss Annette Kellerman put over today at a benefit performance . . . no one suspected her of being a Prima Ballerina.' *Variety* reported that 'the surprise hit of the Metropolitan Show War Benefit was Annette Kellerman in the *Swan Dance*'. And she says in 'My Story' that she never forgot Daniel Frohman telling her 'what a versatile and artistic girl you are'.

The Metropolitan benefit was probably the closest she ever came to the world her mother envisioned for her. It was only because the show was produced by a theatrical impresario rather than a legitimate opera manager that she was able to step over into this world for a night. The experience was to remain with her forever and gave her a taste for charity work which never left her. When she was young and at the height of her popularity, benefits and charity work were a compliment—she was asked because people would pay large sums to see her and she was able to mingle in the highest society both on and off the stage. In later years, when people no longer remembered her so well and her theatrical appearances were dwindling, charity and war work were a way of getting back on stage.

It was not until *A Daughter of the Gods* first appeared and Charles E. Dillingham approached her about appearing at the famous New York Hippodrome that Annette really felt she had reached the pinnacle of her vaudeville career.

Dillingham was one of the top Broadway producers of the day, and the Hippodrome one of the largest and most prestigious theatres in town. Built in 1905, it was designed by Architect J.H. Morgan and, though it was demolished in World War II, it is still considered one of the true wonders of theatre architecture. The stage was twelve times bigger than that of any other Broadway theatre and could hold as many as a thousand performers at a time, or a full-sized circus with elephants and horses. It seated 5140 people and had an 8000 gallon clear glass water tank that could be raised from below the stage by hydraulic pistons. The success of *A Daughter of the Gods* meant Dillingham gave Annette free rein to design her own set. Basically, with Dillingham as executive producer, she was producing, directing and designing her own show on the biggest stage in town. Her idea was to convey the exotic locations of her films on stage. She decided to replicate the famous waterfall scene from *A Daughter of the Gods.*

Downstage, Annette had installed a series of glass-fronted tanks where, as she described it in 'My Story', 'frogs and other sea creatures, only seen in fairlytales, disported themselves'. Flying ballet girls, dressed as glow-worms, flew back and forth making a shadow play on a wide screen where fish were projected. The tanks were decorated with coral and rocks and seaweed and, behind them all on the back wall, a giant waterfall cascaded from the flies down to a huge sunken pool centre stage. Yet again, Annette trained girls to act and swim as mermaids while she, as the Queen of the Mermaids, had her own huge glass-fronted tank. At one point in the show, she slid down a long chute and splashed into the main tank. But it was in the last scene that Annette truly triumphed:

> A large glass tank set in the centre of the stage drove the other settings from sight and memory, and the throng that had assembled to see her dive leaned forward in anticipation. The stage was dark save for the illuminated tank and a powerful ray of light from above which revealed the nymph standing on a springboard high above the tank to the right and, clad in clinging bright maroon silk. As the spectators began to applaud she leaped backward 40 feet into the water.

At the Hippodrome there was no one 'headliner'—everyone was a star in their own right. She was appearing on a bill that included the lovely Charlotte (skating queen and Pavlova of the ice), Sophie Barnard who sang 'Poor Butterfly'—Raymond Hubbell's hit number—and 'that most famous and most gracious wielder of the baton, John Philip Sousa'. Most thrilling of all was that Pavlova, the famous ballerina, was also appearing. Ironically, Annette's show was so popular that Pavlova's 45 minute

spot had to be cut down to eighteen. But the Russian bore her
no grudge. They became firm friends when Annette confided
an unlikely insecurity regarding her hands. Pavlova reassured
her, telling her that she too had always felt her hands were too
big. In the end, though, Annette proved too popular for her idol.
Variety reported:

> Surrounded by a gorgeous setting of a miniature Niagara and
> a grotto, Annette Kellerman replaced Pavlova as the star
> attraction in *The Big Show* at the Hippodrome. While the music
> played and the singers sang and the fish and flying fairies did
> twists and turns in the grotto and the mermaids swam about
> in adjoining tanks, Kellerman did her dives into the centre
> water receptacle. It's the most imposing set Miss Kellerman has
> ever had on stage.

In all, there were 200 mermaids, water nymphs and sprites
as well as all the Hippodrome chorus girls. Songs were specially
written by the popular musical composer Raymond Hubbell.
Jimmie had arranged a contract with Dillingham and Fox at the
same time—Annette was being paid $2000 a week at the
Hippodrome and for her next film with Fox, *Queen of the Sea*, she
was to receive a salary *and* a percentage of the profits. 'On all
sides of Broadway Mr Dillingham is being congratulated on his
wisdom in selecting Miss Kellerman and again restoring a water
spectacle to the big playhouse,' said the *New York Telegraph*.

A photograph from the show reveals that Annette achieved
her aims—with massive waterfalls and thousands of extras, it
looks more like a Busby Berkley movie than a theatre set.

At last Annette was admired by the people she had looked
up to for all those years in vaudeville. When John Philip Sousa,

the famous band leader and composer of *The Stars and Stripes Forever*, told her that he had seen both her films and 'they were the most artistic I've ever seen', and then added, 'May I tell you that you are my favourite picture star?' she was quite overcome.

The Big Show was a huge hit, and Annette remained at the Hippodrome for the next six months. She got to know Sousa rather well and they had a lot of fun preparing for the big Hippodrome parade through the streets of New York. Charles Dillingham asked Annette to head the parade. It was an honour only given to the most popular Broadway stars. Riding on a prancing white mare and wearing a white riding suit with matching kid gaiters and a panama hat, she was followed by Sousa and his big brass band. There were floats with Neptune and his daughter and others with fairytale characters all inspired by Annette's set in *The Big Show*.

On 4 May 1917, the show changed its name for one night to *The Annette Kellerman Night*, not, as one wit put it, because 'the audience is meant to wear less clothes than usual', but because it was to be the Hippodrome's farewell to Annette. In the audience that night were nearly 1500 patrons from Easton, Pennsylvania. This is the town was where the 'Australian Amphritite' had been sent by B.F. Keith for an out of town try-out before her first appearance as a headliner in New York. The Eastoners had never forgotten their first encounter with Annette and regarded her as a native daughter. 'Not that Miss Kellerman expects her admirers to bring flowers, but she does promise to dive for any bouquets that may be tossed over the footlights,' said the *New York Telegraph*.

When not rehearsing or performing, Annette found time to design and build a house with Jimmie in the very swish suburb of Douglas Manor on Long Island—very modern and, with its central fireplace, even a little bit Frank Lloyd Wright. Henry MacMahon of *Motion Picture Classic* reported:

Everything they are interested in is found right at their front door. Across the road is a diving pier and a yacht dock. The house resembles a 'Perfecto' cigar box and the two wings smaller boxes. In the centre is the great living hall with its immense fireplace and the walls hung with trophies of the owner's athletic exploits.

MacMahon interviewed Annette at her new home and found her 'in private life the least affected of her sex and profession— entirely free of the usual "actress-star" haughtiness and freaks of temper. She possesses the modesty that knows no evil.' And he was unable to hide his favourable impression of her physique: 'Her lithe body is the instrument of her amazing athletic virtuosity, just as the pianist's fingers are the instrument of his skill.'

It seems strange that the Sullivans decided to set roots down in one place permanently. Though magazines ran photos of Annette on the lawn at her home pushing little Coo-ee around in a wheelbarrow and looking very rustic and domesticated, the Sullivans never stayed anywhere for too long.

As soon as *The Big Show* finished Annette returned to the Keith circuit and began touring the country in her totally revitalised act. She took as many elements from *The Big Show* as she could on tour, including a ballet act with Russian dancer Edmund Mikalef, wire walking and a little monologue that proved very popular. According to the reporter from the *Milwaukee Missouri News* 'the major interest of the act was furnished by the water woman's clever patter. It's of the breezy English Music Hall type but more subtle in its appeal'. The act also included sixteen numbers sung by two leads and a chorus of 'Kellerman Girls', all directed by Annette. Though pleased that she was 'demonstrating unsuspected versatility', most critics were still convinced that it was as 'a water witch that her perfect figure, grace and skill were fully displayed in diving and swimming with lights designed to show every movement of her slim lithe body'. *Variety* magazine tried to work out why she was still so popular:

> Why has Annette Kellerman become one of the greatest acts in vaudeville, while all—yes ALL other acts are just diving acts and usually close the show. Kellerman is no longer billed as the most perfectly formed woman in the world. The novelty of a glass tank is over. Every carnival is there with aquatic maids. Yet Kellerman keeps them all a thousand miles away.

It was not enough for her to be one of the biggest stars of vaudeville, however: Annette Kelllerman was now to become the first person ever to dive from an aeroplane without a parachute. *Photoplay* reported that: 'The machine was brought within 40 feet of the ocean and down she went.' Though the height she dived from was not a challenge for Annette—she had dived more than once from 90 feet—she had never done it from a moving plane. At the time, even the act of taking off in a flying machine was still considered extremely risky, if not death-defying. But balancing on the canvas wings of a flimsy aeroplane was exactly the sort of challenge Annette thrived on.

At this time she forged ahead with several new money-making propositions. She published her book *Physical Beauty: How to Keep It* in 1918, and there was a plan to make a documentary for women, featuring health and beauty hints and depicting the lives of women in other countries. Sol Lesser, who ran First National Pictures and was Charlie Chaplin's producer, formed a company to produce these and other mainstream Annette Kellerman films. He was proposing to spend close to $600 000 on the film which would become *What Women Love*. Ever since she had begun in 1909, Annette had continued to give her health and beauty lectures and would always include these when touring the vaudeville circuit. Since the release of *A Daughter of the Gods*, she had been writing weekly articles that were syndicated across the country, urging municipal councils to build swimming pools, as 'adequate public bathing facilities will make an improvement of from 10 to 17 per cent in the health of any community of 30 000 people or more'.

It was at this time, just after the end of World War I, that Mipps, who was about to leave Paris for Australia, was telegrammed on a whim by her sister to come quickly to America. When she arrived, Annette was nowhere to be seen. She was filming in Yosemite National Park. Now lost, the film was one of those financed by Sol Lesser, an educational picture showing women how to keep healthy, which was shot in the exotic locations of the national park. A reporter from *Picture Play Magazine*, arriving in Yosemite for a holiday, was immediately reeled in by Jimmie to interview his wife:

> Miss Kellerman was discovered sitting on the end of a high diving board above the Camp Yosemite swimming pool. She told me hospitably to 'come right on up'. She edged me over so as to let me sit right on the end of the board, though I demurred politely. She was wearing a blue mandarin coat over her bathing suit and a cap of blue rubberized silk covered her hair.

Their *tête à tête* was interrupted by Jimmie calling out to her 'that the cameraman had got into range and that she could dive anytime she wanted. He called her "Tootie" and she called him

"Hon".' After the first take, she reclined by the side of the pool and confided to the reporter:

> People often say to me that I must have a great talent for doing the things I do—but I didn't, everything that I have learned came hard . . . fencing, golf, wire walking, riding and ballet dancing—any woman can learn some of these things, especially if they see my pictures with slow movements.

The film included Annette wire walking across a waterfall. When the reporter gasped, she continued:

> Oh yes I suppose it *was* dangerous but I balanced alright, though the wind was so high that I had to throw away my Japanese umbrella and trust to my own devices. Then I drove a golf ball from Overhanging Rock and we'll call that 'the longest drive in the world', because it's over four thousand feet straight downward that measured into yards would take the cake, wouldn't it?
>
> 'Sorry Tootie,' came Friend Husband's apologetic voice, 'but the light's too poor for the swimming scene. We'll have to shoot'em tomorrow.'
>
> 'Righto!' said Annette amiably. 'In that case I'll come out of the swim and dress for dinner.'

This article provides a rare view of their married life from the outside and reveals a happy relationship, but still Annette, as always, is the star and Jimmie her ever-ready assistant.

When finished, the films were shown on her vaudeville tours and proved very popular. As the *New York Times* noted: 'each movement and position of the diver's performance is brought out by the slow motion camera, and it is fascinating to observe what the eye would ordinarily miss.'

After shooting the film, Annette came back to Santa Monica with Jimmie. They rented a house there with a court and she took up tennis with a vengeance. She had been a very competitive social player but now she began taking lessons with May Sutton, pioneer Davis Cup player, and Wimbledon champion Suzanne Lenglen. She worked at her game until she was good enough to play professionally with her teachers. A photograph of her taken around this time has the caption: 'Diving Venus as good at the nets as she is in the water. The president of the Los Angeles Tennis Club presenting a cup to Miss Annette Kellerman, winner of the tennis tournament in this city.' When she had to leave Los Angeles to tour the vaudeville circuit, she was so stuck on the game that she told her sister 'I cannot let tennis go', and hired a young man with a salary and all expenses paid just to play tennis with for two hours a day.

The tour was from West to East, and Mipps and her husband Fred Wooster came along for the ride. Mipps reports that they began with a drive through the Mohave Desert 'among all those terrifying looking cacti popping up on all sides'. In accordance with Annette's love of driving, they covered huge distances. From the desert they travelled south to New Orleans, Moulin Rouge, Memphis, up the Missouri to Kansas and St Louis, across to Canada, Winnipeg, Calgary, Edmonton, Vancouver, Columbia and Seattle, back to Santa Monica and then San Francisco.

Annette was in constant motion—nothing could stop her. She wrote, dived, swam, danced, sang, played tennis, toured and drove until one day she finally came to a halt. There was nowhere to go anymore.

It was in Chicago on the final leg of a tour of the country that her agent told her that vaudeville was no more. Theatres all over the country had been completely taken over by movies. She could have as much work as she liked, but vaudeville theatre owners could no longer afford to tour her *Big Show*. They offered her a spot for a very short act before a movie was screened—it was back to the bad old days of four shows a day. Annette says in 'My Story' that she made her decision on the spur of the moment: 'Without a qualm I said: "No thanks, we've worked hard and saved our money Jimmie and I. No four shows a day."' Annette wanted to go home, to Australia.

Sailing into Sydney Harbour on the SS *Ventura* was wonderful for Annette after an absence of so many years. It was 1921, and she hadn't been back since she left to swim the Channel in 1904. The harbour and the city looked magnificent, and the dock was crowded with well-wishers and fans. She was returning to perform at the new Royal Theatre and there was a star's welcome for her, including a brass band. Annette and Mipps had promised themselves that their first drive in Sydney would be in a hansom cab. When she left Australia seventeen years before the hansom cab had always seemed the height of sophistication to Annette and her younger sister who rarely, if ever, had the chance to ride in one. To the astonishment of the organisers of the civic reception at the Town Hall, they did just that, followed by cars and a parade on foot.

Unfortunately those who had brought her and the full company out to tour had neglected to tell them that renovations to the Theatre Royal weren't quite completed. Her Majesty's, nearby on the corner of Pitt and Market Streets, underneath the plush George's Hotel, was the only other theatre big enough, but was booked out for another month.

Annette, undaunted, hired a house at Potts Point, overlooking the harbour, and rehearsed and reminisced. Finally her tour organisers booked her into the Tivoli, the most famous vaudeville theatre in town and one that, as children, Annette and her siblings were forbidden to set foot in. Now she was up on the stage playing to packed houses and gaining new fans. Annette won them over, and even made lifelong friends of some who could make or break an artist—described by Mipps as the notorious 'First Nighters' and 'Gallery Girls'.

From Melbourne, the show went on tour to Adelaide, then down to Hobart. Annette was popular everywhere, and always played to full houses. Next she toured New Zealand. Mipps, who went along with them, remembers 'arriving in what seemed to be a deserted village, with only the town dog scratching the dust in the middle of the road'. The local hall was empty apart from the village goat clearing up the rubbish inside. It seemed there would be no audience that night, but according to Mipps there was 'no need to worry—they came on horseback, in cars, carts, trucks, on foot, any old how. The hall was always packed and the little ones were brought in, squatting on the floor. She had the same exhilarating reception from Auckland to Christchurch.'

Annette returned to the United States in 1923. With the decline in vaudeville, Annette found herself at a loose end and decided to open a health food shop in San Diego. She'd always been interested in food and nutrition, and had begun to study with Dr Kellogg, a fellow vegetarian, at the University of California. She was living in Santa Monica and would drive to the store every day. She still saw her friends from the film industry, and entertained them at her home. But running a health food store, studying with Dr Kellogg and entertaining friends was never going take the place of vaudeville. Annette decided to leave America for Europe and England, where variety and music hall were still alive and well.

13
CONQUERING THE CONTINENT

It was 1925 when the Sullivans returned to England, spending three years there with Annette playing the largest English vaudeville or musical hall circuit—the Stoll. Oscar Stoll had built the famous London Coliseum in 1904 and Annette made eight appearances there this time. It was a huge theatre which could seat 2558 people. Built in the Renaissance style with an enormous tower, it was topped by the famous globe which revolved with the letters 'Coliseum' lit up. There were several tea rooms in various parts of the building, an immense 'Baronial Smoking Hall' complete with first-class bars, several so-called 'retiring rooms' and even a post office where telegrams and telephone messages could be left or dispatched. There was also the usual conservatory and a fernery. The biggest wonder of all was the 'King's Car', described on the British Library website:

> The Royal party will step into a richly furnished lounge, which,
> at a signal, will move softly along a track formed in the floor,
> through a salon into a large foyer, which contains the entrance

to the Royal Box. The Lounge-Car remains in position at the entrance to the Box and serves as an ante-room during the performance.

Unfortunately, when King Edward visited the Coliseum and was led into the 'King's Car' amid some ceremony, the car blew a fuse and wouldn't move, so the King, roaring with laughter, made his way to the Royal Box on foot.

Backstage, things were just as revolutionary—the first moving stage in England had been installed to speed up the change time between acts. One act could have its stage set while another was performing out front. It was on this revolving stage that Annette became a big hit in London. She recalls the shows she did there as her finest.

Here Annette performed her wire act number. The wire was stretched across the stage and she used small dolls that were replicas of famous movie stars of the time (including Buster Keaton, Mae Marsh, Charlie Chaplin and Mary Pickford). They were about 3 feet high. Annette's wire was 7 feet above the stage and the dolls were hung on an invisible wire attached underneath. The figures danced to the same tempo as she did when she danced on her wire. 'The effect was unusual and drew much comment and many laughs,' she wrote.

It took a great deal of skill to make the act work. Wearing her tight-fitting, red, white and green Columbine costume, with a short skirt hung with matching bobbles, Annette climbed the ladder and, balancing with the aid of her Chinese paper umbrella, danced back and forth along the wire, making it look as easy as a walk in the park. One night, as she nimbly pranced above the admiring crowd, the wire broke. The audience gasped as Annette fell and hit the bare stage, landing in a crumpled heap amongst her little dolls. The curtain came down and the auditorium was hushed, the crowd not knowing whether Annette was unconscious or worse. But according to Jimmie, who was watching as usual in the wings, 'she just got up and shook herself like a little chicken', dashed through the curtains to the bewildered crowd and called out: 'Here we go again!' There was terrific laughter and applause and the incident made the morning papers. She performed two shows a day at the Coliseum, and the theatre was always full. She loved the British audiences and they loved her, feeling she was almost one of them.

It was while she was performing at the London Coliseum that Annette was spotted by the manager of the Scala Theatre in Berlin, who asked whether she would be willing to perform the same act at his theatre. He had seen her doing what she called her 'gym' or 'physical culture act'. Combining serious exercise with humorous tricks, she showed women how to do ordinary everyday housework in extraordinary ways. Annette described it as:

> a sort of burlesque of housework and I do everything according
> to physical culture rules. I pick up things from the floor without
> bending my knees and, dust the chandelier with my feet while
> standing on my head and use lamps like dumbbells.

It was very funny, and particularly appealed to the European audiences. 'Of course you will do the act in German,' the manager of the Scala told Annette. In 'My Story' Annette writes that she spoke fluent German and said 'Sure, that will be great fun.' Mipps, recalling the same event in her own memoirs, said that her sister 'just about knowing "Guten Abend", set about learning the whole script word for word from a teacher'. Her first night made the New York papers:

The famous mermaid on making her first appearance of her
life in Berlin the other night got the biggest hand of the evening
from the huge audience when it was announced it was the first
time in her life she had spoken German on stage and was
enjoying herself.

While in Berlin, she was approached by the director of the
Scala Theatre in Copenhagen asking her to come there and
perform the gym act in Danish. She was definitely not fluent
in Danish, but that didn't bother Annette who set about studying
the language at the Berlitz School.

From then on, the whole thing just ricocheted—in
Copenhagen she was approached by the Zeigfeld of Sweden,
Earnest Rolfe, asking her to come to Stockholm. 'But you must
do your act in Swedish,' he told her, 'And do some comedy with
me.' So Annette began to learn Swedish. In Sweden they were
delighted that she had taken the trouble to perform in their
language. From Sweden she went to Norway, then Rotterdam
and The Hague. This was a real test for Annette, as she says in
'My Story' that she found Dutch 'a truly horrible language to
learn and speak'. But she conquered the language and the
audiences so completely that the Rotterdam newspaper wrote: 'It
is a pity that the Dutch artists on the programme did not take
a few lessons from Annette Kellerman. We understood
everything she said but our own artists could not be heard
beyond the third row.' Ironically, one of the comedians on the
bill had to translate the article for her because Annette only knew
enough of the language to get through the dialogue in her act.

Altogether, Annette and Jimmie spent eight years in Europe,
often accompanied by her sister and brother-in-law, Fred.
Annette and Jimmie would stay in the best hotels while Mipps

and Fred preferred the common touch. The tours in Europe were not as intense as they had been in America. Annette, used to spending most of the day and half the night in the theatre, eating her main meal at 11 p.m. and sleeping when she could, had time to actually look around. In Deauville, while the Sullivans stayed at the famous Hermitage Hotel, which Mipps described as 'the very last word in high class', Mipps and Fred stayed in a family resort down the road. At the hotel, Annette mingled with models and designers of haute couture and met celebrities of the day like Maurice Chevalier and Coco Chanel. Annette loved it and fitted in perfectly, 'with her trunks of stunning clothing'. But she and Jimmie did enjoy escaping the merry-go-round and visiting Mipps and Fred 'for a good old Aussie picnic'.

They dug mussels on the beach at low tide and made a fire to cook them. Sitting on the sand with baguettes and red wine, eating their mussels they found themselves surrounded by curious locals. Mipps reported their comments in 'Let's Do Something': 'Venez voir!' they said. 'Would you believe it they are having their dèjeuner. Poor things!'

While in Europe, Annette attracted the attention of fans wherever she went. One in particular, heiress and film starlet Dorothy Kidd, followed her all the way across the continent. Jimmie was asked many times what it was like being married to a celebrity. 'How about the wolves?' they asked him. 'Sure, there were wolves at the door many times but Annette didn't like wolves,' he replied. One admirer kept accidentally on purpose running into them all over Europe, hoping to get rid of Jimmie and spend some time with Annette. Annette showed the man a photo of five kids and told him: 'These are our children in the USA.' They never saw him again.

14
WE'LL BE BEACHCOMBERS

When Jimmie and Annette returned again to Australia in the early 1930s, Annette was still welcomed as a celebrity. She was interviewed by a news crew and, though she would have been in her mid-forties, she appears very young and fit, and is quite mischievous. She looks very chic in a beret, tight-fitting twin set and checked trousers. Speaking in a rather cultivated stagey accent, not American but not really Australian either, she was definitely not camera shy, telling the cameraman quite brazenly that she was off to stay on an island and was going to be completely nude. She was speaking about the Great Barrier Reef, a tropical paradise in North Queensland.

The first time Annette had become interested in the Barrier Reef was in London in 1926, during the General Strike. All her performances were cancelled and, with Mipps and Fred and Jimmie, she spent the nine days sightseeing in London. On cold days they visited the centrally heated museums. 'We would stand entranced by the Great Barrier Reef cases and books in the library,' wrote Mipps. Annette was instantly hooked on the untouched beauty of the place. Then and there, she began to write a book for children, *Fairy Tales of the South Seas,* which naturally contained adventure stories set in the waters around an imagined tropical paradise. 'We all four vowed we'd go to the Barrier Reef to see if it all was true,' Mipps wrote in 'Let's Do Something'.

Now the Sullivans were ready to make that trip. They joined Mipps and Fred and drove from Widgee in south Queensland, where Fred's parents' property was, up to the Barrier Reef as planned. The roads in the early 1930s were horrendous, with nothing on either side but virgin bush. Along the way they camped, got caught in a flood 'for a week or two' and then went to stay on Lindeman Island for fifteen months. In the local launch and in flat-bottomed boats, the party of four island-hopped from one pristine setting to another.

Even on holiday in the middle of nowhere, Annette and Jimmie were still plotting the next move in her fading career. Camping on each island for a few nights, they took pictures or films of everything, though it was difficult to film underwater because of the lime content of the coral. They made a short film about a sea-nymph who captures a mermaid's water baby with Annette playing both the mermaid and the nymph. When they returned to America they took this film and others they had made back with them. Calling them 'swimologues' it seems they were trying to get them played as shorts before the feature. Jimmie and Annette told B.R. Chrysler of the *Toledo Blade* that they wanted to make 'a subaqueous picture in which she will lead twenty-five girls in a routine similar to those executed by the Music Hall Rockettes'. The picture never eventuated.

The three Australians were happy on the islands, but city-bred Jimmie thought they were all nuts to enjoy being uncomfortable with no amenities. However, as usual, 'Whatever he thought he complied with grace as he always did with Annette,' said Mipps. Jimmie was also the only one of the four who couldn't swim and, despite living on islands surrounded by water for fifteen months, refused to learn. Perhaps it was his only rebellion against a wife for whom he was willing to give up so much. Though he couldn't swim, he spent hours underwater in a diving bell filming Annette.

On one camping trip they stayed on the neighbouring island of Maher, which was divided from Lindeman by a wide and rapid channel. Accompanied by Dick, a young Tiwi Island Aboriginal boy, they were dropped off there by launch and left with enough provisions for a few days. Almost as soon as they had put up their tents, a cyclone hit and they were stranded there for two weeks. Luckily Dick helped Fred catch some fish because they hadn't brought enough supplies for their unexpectedly long stay. Poor Jimmie, who hated camping at the best of times, was stuck in a tent with a cyclone outside and toothache inside. One night, when the wind was particularly strong, Annette woke up to find him gone. She jumped up to the sound of strange scuffings and stepped out of her tent to see her husband, pyjama pants rolled up, trudging backwards around the fire. He was up to his knees in a trench he had dug to protect the fire in case the island was drenched by huge waves. He looked so serious and determined that no one had the heart to tell him the worst of the storm was over and the trench wouldn't have done much against a cyclonic wave. Like all Annette's adventures, it ended happily. The owner of nearby Hayman Island, Doctor MacDonald, arrived in a launch with a set of dental tools. The doctor fixed Jimmie's teeth and Annette was offered a half-share in the island, which she declined. It later became a very popular and lucrative tourist resort.

After fifteen months of island-hopping, Annette and Jimmie were, '"sashaying" again—thinking, moseying around to see where they could rest their heads', according to Mipps. Even though they were no longer touring, they kept on moving—first to Sydney, where they took a flat overlooking the harbour, then to Canberra, the North Coast and up to where Mipps and Fred had taken a lease on their own Barrier Reef island—Newry.

It was back to the United States in 1937 and straight down to Florida to avoid the winter. 'Immediately,' Annette writes in 'My Story', 'I was approached by the Elk Club in Palm Beach to stage a marine fantasy at the Palm Beach Bath and Tennis Club.' There's never much small talk in 'My Story'—departures and arrivals and other huge life changes always happen immediately and are dealt with swiftly and with little fuss— very much as the author dealt with her own life. Before the marine fantasy, Jimmie and Annette had been filming an adagio. The underwater footage Jimmie had taken of Annette on the Barrier Reef had not worked out as well as they'd hoped, so they decided to try filming at Silver Springs in Florida. The footage still survives—the water is crystal clear and Annette at 51 is remarkable underwater—precise, balletic and with a cheeky smile for the cameraman. In this beautiful performance it is possible to see how far she had come from her early swimming days, where she thrilled the crowds by simply swimming freestyle in a pool and making a few basic dives. Her movements are graceful and mesmerising, and it is clear she has truly combined sport and art and created a new an art form—underwater ballet.

It was in Silver Springs that they met President Roosevelt, who was there to exercise his polio-stricken legs in the famous spring waters. Having heard of Annette's crippled childhood, he sent for her to discuss the benefits of water for his legs, and

Mipps describes in 'Let's Do Something' how Annette spent the afternoon with him and devised some exercises that he found very helpful. The president was not the only person to benefit from Annette's experience. In the 1930s while she was in Australia she advised Sister Elizabeth Kenny. Frowned on by the medical establishment, Sister Kenny was renowned for opening Australia's first polio clinic in 1933 and was using her own controversial methods with tremendous success in the treatment of polio victims.

After the demise of vaudeville, Annette's only performances were for charity. She enjoyed it immensely and it kept her up on the stage and in the limelight, even if that light was slightly dimmer. The Palm Beach Bath and Tennis Club had an exclusive membership, 'She had the millionaires behind her and *carte blanche* to go ahead,' said Jimmie, and produced a benefit show for children with infantile paralysis. Ever since her early days in films she had wanted to do an outdoor water pageant. It was created on Palm Beach and people came from all over the state to see King Neptune arriving on board his ship with his escort of mermaids.

The President and Mrs Roosevelt came over from Silver Springs to watch, and the entertainment continued on a huge stage, especially built for the occasion, on the beach. Annette insisted 'nothing like it has ever been seen before nor has its like been seen since.' It was in the same year, 1937, that flamboyant theatrical entrepreneur Billy Rose produced his first aquacade in Cleveland. Rose went on to make extravagant shows throughout the late 1930s and early 1940s, introducing the world to swimming stars like Johnny Weissmuller and Esther Williams. While Annette was creating her pageants for charity, Rose was making millions. She must have seen his shows on subsequent trips to the States and was apparently not too impressed, writing in 'My Story':

> My water shows in no way conflict with any aquacade on stage or screen. As originator of this type of show my ideas are entirely different from what has been done along these lines and what really can be done with this type of show.

As the inventor of water ballet and what was to become synchronised swimming, she found it difficult to stand by and watch others take her ideas in directions she'd never thought of and didn't enjoy. Though she never spoke of it, there must have been some disappointment in not being asked to participate in these new aquacades. Perhaps at 50 she was feeling just a little *passé*.

But Annette, never feeling sorry for herself for long, was on the move again. This time she was homesick. 'Let's go back to Aussie,' she said to Jimmie. 'We'll be a couple of beachcombers.' They returned to Australia in 1939 and put the world behind them, this time retreating again to the beauty and calm of Newry Island.

Unlike the very tropical islands closer to Cairns and farther from the coast, Newry is lower down, near Mackay at the south end of the Barrier Reef. It is wild and windswept, with rocky exposed headlands and sandstone cliffs. Today it is still a rather pristine wilderness with no hotels. In the early 1930s when Fred and Mipps took over the lease, it must have seemed miles from nowhere. Just outside her front door Annette could have seen koalas, bandicoots and echidnas. And in the sky an amazing variety of birds, including brahminy kites, ospreys and white-bellied sea eagles soared above the coast while noisy pittas and rose-crowned pigeons nested in the rainforest.

No doubt Annette would have explored the whole island thoroughly, while Jimmie, without a piano or his beloved paperwork, read a book or pottered around the house.

Kitch Robinson, who as a young girl lived on neighbouring Rabbit Island, remembers Annette well, but was much closer to her sister. She thought that Annette acted the part of a movie star. Legend has it that Annette would swim the shark-infested channel to go shopping and then hitch a ride back on the next boat. It could have been possible, as the closest point on Newry was 3 miles away from Seaforth, the nearest town on the mainland. It's certainly true that Annette went swimming every day, and though she was out of the habit of long-distance swimming, there's no reason why she wouldn't have loved the challenge. It could have only have been done in the winter months though, because in summer the channel was, and still is, filled with estuarine crocodiles and box jellyfish that can kill or paralyse.

Annette could not relax, not even on a tropical island holiday—she behaved there as though it was one big rehearsal for the next phase of her career. Although she couldn't have known it at the time, when war broke out that's exactly what happened—a whole new world opened up. In the year she stayed on Newry Island, she took up the piano accordion, wrote twenty songs and finished and published the book she had begun in London, *Fairy Tales of the South Seas*. According to Mipps, who did the illustrations, the book was 'half biography, half fantasy'. The main protagonists of the tales were always brave swimmers and divers or mermaids who risked their lives to save an errant family member or, in some cases, entire villages. One heroine was crippled as a child and learning to swim not only cured her but allowed her to save the village from impending disaster. Marion Arnott, the child of a family friend, remembers Annette really liking children; she sent her and her sister June a copy of her fairytales with the inscription: 'To my darling little friends with love from Annette.' They both thought *Fairy Tales of the South Seas* was wonderful. Today the stories seem a little laboured, with the representation of the indigenous island people very much a product of the times— rather condescending and sometimes racist.

Annette never really left the limelight, not even on Newry— 'being with my sister and having the most perfect scenery for my stage, I felt I was a star indeed,' she wrote in 'My Story'. She continued to keep herself fit and was never idle. A photo of her on Newry shows her in shorts and a matching midriff top walking a tight rope slung between two palm trees, lithe as a teenager. 'The years had left me in perfect health,' she wrote, and also noted that she weighed the same as she had at the height of her career. Snorkelling every day on the reef, she would dive to a depth of 30 feet. These underwater interludes provided inspiration for her fairytales.

After their last trip, camping on Lindeman Island, Newry, though equally remote, seemed positively luxurious, especially to Jimmy. Fred had built them a beautiful little house out of rocks from the beach. The foundations are still there today, and the Queensland Environment and Protection Agency is in the process of putting up a plaque to commemorate the spot.

Jimmy and Annette continued to return to Newry until Mipps and her husband left in the 1950s. On one trip there in 1949, on a train bound for Mackay, they struck up a conversation with R. Emerson Curtis. 'Our home and work are in New York but we spend parts of each year, when it is possible, at Newry,' Annette told him. She and Jimmie also told him they wished they could stay there forever 'because it has everything for perfect happiness'.

Jimmie was Annette's anchor—no matter what she wanted to do or where she wanted to go, he was there waiting as a safe harbour. It is interesting to speculate whether she would have been such a risk-taker, so free of fear and convention, if she had married someone more like herself.

But they couldn't stay cut off from the world forever. It was on Newry that the Sullivans and the Woosters heard about the fall of France. From their haven in the middle of the Coral Sea, they heard Churchill's speeches crackle over the short-wave radio. Suddenly, as Mipps recalled, the adventure was over: 'The news came in so swiftly, all of it bad, we were a sober lot.'

15
THE DINKUM DIGGERS' DIP

Though the war was being waged far from Australia, and particularly from Newry Island, Annette, like many others, felt that she had to do something. On the long trip back to Sydney, over 2000 miles, she and Jimmie decided on a way they could help the war effort. They came up with the idea of the 'Red Cross Theatrical Unit', or RCTU, the only one of its kind. It would raise money for the Red Cross and, almost as importantly, Annette would be back on stage. Fortunately she had brought from the United States, just in case, twelve trunks of costumes and beautiful scenery, described in 'My Story' as 'gorgeous materials, feathers, spangles etc.', that she had collected on her tours around the world. Like most people at the time, Annette believed the war would be a flash in the pan, but she continued her work from 1939 until the end of hostilities and raised over £25 000 for the Red Cross.

Annette took the title of Honorary Director, which gives no idea of the scope of her role. She was in charge of the whole company—directing the Kellermanettes, writing and producing the shows. And there were hundreds of these shows, up and down the east coast of Australia all the way to Port Moresby in New Guinea. Jimmie managed the entire thing and booked the performances. Annette was presented with a whole new audience of soldiers and sailors to entertain. Because it was Jimmie and Annette's money which financed everything, for the first time in her career she had complete artistic control of each and every production.

Betty Paige, who was a teenager at the time, remembers being chosen from a group of office girls to appear in the limelight of wartime performance. The only prerequisite was looking reasonably good in a swimsuit. Highly impressed by Annette, Betty thought she was a handsome woman with a good figure, but recalls the shows being 'pretty bad'. Though the tunes were not all dreadful, some were quite catchy judging by some of the lyrics, Betty Paige may have had good reason for her opinion. The words to the song 'ANZAC' give some idea of Annette's style:

Who's behind the Union Jack? We are.
Who's behind the Empire? Australia.
Australia, Australia you're the land of the Southern Cross.
Australia, Australia you're free as an Albatross.
Australia, Australia you've been here since Captain Cook.
You'll never get out for an Axis crook.
You're at the back of the Union Jack
And we know you'll never crack.
Oh ANZAC ANZAC ANZAC

Jimmie, on the other hand, said in 'My Story', that he believed 'she had written some really fine numbers'. He must have been referring to the music, not the lyrics, of 'The Dinkum Diggers' Dip':

Let's do the Dinkum Diggers' Dip,
Hi diddle de diddle de ti de doo.

Hump yer bluey and hum and holler.
Gallop around like a jackeroo,
Hoppity hop like a kangaroo.

For Annette, the songs were another feather she could add
to her theatrical cap. They were fully orchestrated—sometimes,
though not always, arranged by Annette. The sheet music for
'Spanish Dance' was compiled and arranged for her by David
Cope. It was scored for piano, harp, four first violins, two
violas, two cellos and bass, flute and piccolo, one oboe, one
first and second clarinet, one bassoon, four second horns, one
trombone, one timpani and one set of drums—a 24-piece
orchestra in all.

Described in the program as 'an intimate Musical Revue',
the show was called *We're all In It*. There were twenty numbers,
and Annette was in almost every one of them—dancing solo in
'On Tiptoes', with the Kellermanettes in 'Dinkum Diggers Dip'
and finally with her piano accordion in 'Let's All Get Together'.

Despite finding the show a little old-fashioned, Betty Paige
and the girls enjoyed working with Annette. She was 'really nice,
lovely to us,' Betty said in a 1999 interview. Rehearsals were fun
in the Sullivans' posh harbourside apartment and so were the
performances every night in different suburban town halls.
Wearing big glamorous headdresses, which Betty described as
being 'like the ones you saw in movies when people walked
down the stairs', they danced to the music Annette had written.
As usual, the girls she recruited were non-professional, and
Annette had to make something of them. But the girls in *Neptune's
Daughter* and *A Daughter of the Gods* had been paid; these girls were
not, and the quality of the shows she produced during the war,
no matter how big, was always amateurish.

Marjorie Sherman was one of the ballet dancers Annette took on tours. She recalls that the first time she met Annette she was very excited. She and five other of the most promising dancers from the Mavis Skykes School of Dance had come for a costume fitting and the door was opened by this 'vision dressed in a beautiful floating dress, a small hat pulled on her head and a scarf that floated behind her as she walked, like a ballet dancer'. Marjorie never saw her without the hat, though they often toured together. Some of the girls thought it was because she wore a wig, while others had heard about the accident in *Neptune's Daughter* and imagined gruesome gashes to her face and neck. In fact, the hat hid the scar that was the legacy of her early London diving days, when she cracked her head on the bottom of a shallow pool.

Marjorie and the girls were taken upstairs to an enclosed verandah, according to Marjorie, 'with hanging clothes of every colour and description. It was like being in a drapery store'. While Jimmie stood patiently at the door in case she needed him, Annette then began draping pieces of 'wispy, glittery cloth' around the girls. Most of the girls found Annette rather theatrical and very 1920s, and also rather bossy, so they 'smothered their giggles'. But Marjorie, the youngest, was impressed by Annette, who reminded her of Gloria Swanson—someone else who took control and 'brought life out around herself'. She recalled her still being very supple and able to dance beautifully on her toes.

When America joined the war, Jimmie and Annette were asked by US General Charles M. Derry to work for the troops in a joint American and Australian club, Sydney's Hollywood Canteen. 'For two years we had the unglamorous job of being cooks at the American Centre in Sydney. Jimmie did the hamburgers and I, as Mrs Sullivan, did the eggs. One hundred dozen eggs every Sunday,' Annette said in 'My Story'. June Smith, a family friend, remembered in an interview: 'Cooking eggs for the soldiers was pretty easy. I think it was a case of being seen. Annette liked to keep a high profile.' At five o'clock in the afternoon, when they went home, the Sullivans held open house for the servicemen and patients from the US hospitals. The girls ('My girls' she called them) who performed with Annette all week in different towns and hospitals, were then called in on Sundays to play hostess to the American soldiers. Even Annette admitted (for the first time) that, 'it was a continual round of effort and we kept going at full speed all the time', but there was no shortage of volunteers—she had 60 girls on an active list and another 60 on a waiting list.

As time went by Annette's theatrical ideas became more outdated; nevertheless, knowing no other way of life, she soldiered on. For many years she still received letters from men thanking her for her shows and hospitality. One, Micheal Tomaino, wrote: 'I guess you've adopted yourselves a son.'

Calling herself the 'Aussie Muggsie', Annette's articles now appeared in *Variety*. In these she described the whirlwind tours for American boys far from home in US hospitals and camps across Australia. They performed for the survivors of Guadalcanal and the hit of the show was an original of hers, 'Be My Stick in the Mud and I'll Be your Tootsy Wootsy'. She admitted that the song 'will never make the Dime Store counters but in the wards it's No 1 on the hit parade'. There were around 60 in the troupe, and they played everywhere from 'swell set ups with trimmings' to nothing but a bare shed with a galvanised iron roof—and a rain storm competing with the performance. But nothing could make Annette happier than the being on the road, 'swapping make-up and towels and dressing on a postage stamp. Wotta life, not a dime to show but a million dollar feeling inside.'

Variety readers got her first-hand account of what the Diving Venus had been doing:

> Well she still weighs 125 lbs, feels like the old Hippodrome days—plenty of pep—a mistress of ceremonies, sings a song or two, plays the accordion for sing-along sessions, does whacky monologues about the fleet and army and winds up doing a high kicking dance. The boys give her a great hand!—after all she wasn't a headliner on the greatest vaudeville circuit the world has ever known for years without learning something about show business.

Entertaining the armed forces was just like being a headliner once more, and Annette seems to have had enough 'pep' to keep up the spirits of everyone around her. When she wasn't penning for *Variety* she was writing to 'her boys' or sending letters to celebrities asking them to come out and join her in entertaining the troops. Though her fellow countryman Cecil Kellaway, a big star in Hollywood at the time, regretted that he couldn't come over, Gary Cooper did. There's also a letter from Walt Disney, recalling a meeting with Annette in 1924 and offering an original sketch of Bambi on celluloid to auction for the RCTU. She still had plenty of friends in high places, and her article for *Variety* elicited fond memories from old admirers. One, who describes himself as 'only another fan', never forgot Annette in *Neptune's Daughter*. He wrote that it would be a 'thrill' to get a note from her and signed himself 'Jim, Major Moran MC'. Another of Annette's projects involved organising comics for the American troops. The *Evening News Baltimore* wrote:

> Mothers and fathers of these servicemen will remember Miss Annette Kellerman who was born in Australia, as the 'Perfect

Woman'. Soldiers and sailors in Australia know her today as Mrs James Sullivan who organises shows to entertain them: as the Red Cross worker who comes to visit them and as the lady who brings them the American funny papers.

Touring up and down the coast, Annette was still popular, and even a little controversial. In the northern New South Wales town of Lismore it was reported 'Miss Kellerman put the crowd into good humour with her wisecracks at the expense of the civic authorities'. She promised that on her next tour she would dazzle them with her Water Follies at the Lismore Memorial Baths.

It was during wartime that Annette created her *Musical Marine Phantasy* at the North Sydney Olympic Pool—a big event to raise funds for the Royal Prince Alfred Hospital. Annette had more than 200 well-known swimmers and over 2000 people attended. It was *the* event on the Sydney social calendar. The *Sunday Guardian Sun* wrote:

> Five hundred elaborate costumes were brought from America by Miss Kellerman. Amongst the most notable was one sewn with five hundred pearls worn by Miss Kellerman. Each pearl cost a dollar. Glamourous girls in white brassiere costumes laced with glittering silver, white floodlights turned the water to rainbow hues, drew tumultous applause. The high dives and swimming by 40 girls in glittering gold sequences provided one of the outstanding numbers, *In Neptune's Garden*. Water solos, including underwater swimming by Miss Kellerman were the highlights of several items.

Newsreel footage shows rehearsals where Annette is marching behind a line of girls perched on the edge of the pool about to dive. As she passes each one, she clicks her fingers and, like clockwork, they dive in a falling line. One of the 25 swimmers and divers in the show, Joanna Baulken, recalls having to dive in on the exact beat of the music, coming up to the surface with hands joined she said: 'She was a marvellous teacher, a perfectionist who had all our seaweed costumes and caps covered in sequins sent from New York.' June Smith, who was also in the show, though not as a featured diver or swimmer, remembers: 'We all had to wear jazzy costumes. Most of the outfit was the headgear that stuck out of the water.' Once in the pool, the girls in the water formed a map of Australia and had to keep very still, 'if you moved you ruined it,' said June's sister, Marion Arnott, who was a ballet dancer on a floating pontoon behind the synchronised swimmers. They both remember it as being a very exciting and 'lavish' evening. The grand finale was never forgotten by Joanna Baulken: 'A tightrope was tightened across the swimming pool. Annette Kellerman, who still had the figure of a young girl, though she was in her fifties, wore a stunning white satin swimsuit.' With a little umbrella held high above her head, she walked across the width of the North Sydney Olympic Pool.

When the war finally ended Annette and Jimmie both felt a little let down, although their work hadn't gone unappreciated. 'Jimmie and I had nothing to show . . . but letters and the grand feeling that we left nothing undone to help others during those terrible years,' Annette wrote in 'My Story'. The Commonwealth of Australia thanked them for their help and the American National Red Cross recognised services faithfully performed. In 1944, a wing in the new King George Hospital, 'The Annette Kellerman Wing', was named after her. She was presented with flag of the American Red Cross and managed to get it signed by all the her friends in the top American brass, including Generals Eisenhower and Macarthur and her friend President

Harry Truman, whom she recalled in the *Gold Coast News* as being 'a dear little man'.

After all their hard work, all the Sullivans wanted was to go back to the United States. They looked forward to a long and relaxing journey home. All ships had been requisitioned, but finally they were notified of a berth on the SS *Mariposa*. Annette and Jimmie found out that they were travelling with 750 war brides and their 350 babies. The minute they set foot on the ship, the captain press-ganged them into organising the entertainment for the voyage. The exhausted Annette 'buckled down' and in no time produced *The Mariposa Merrymakers*. Inevitably, she and Jimmie also ended up looking after the brides and their babies. It was a difficult job because, though most of the brides were thrilled and happy at the prospect of life in America, in the middle of the long journey others had a change of heart and at each port there would be attempted escapes in Fiji, Okinawa and Hawaii. The captain, however, had promised to deliver 750 brides. The ship would have to stay in port until the crew had scoured each city to bring back the errant brides. Annette recalled years later that it was 'the most god awful awful trip of my life'. Arriving in San Francisco, the Sullivans kept a very low profile. They decided they didn't want to discuss their work in Australia 'that was for the soldiers, not us . . . we just lost ourselves until Abe Lastfogel dug us up,' Annette said.

16
A NAMBY PAMBY ATTEMPT

Abe Lastfogel was a legendary talent scout at the William Morris Agency from 1912 to 1984. His USO Camp Shows, with over 7000 performers, were on a scale that Annette could only dream of. Two hundred million servicemen were entertained by Dinah Shore, James Cagney, Gary Cooper, James Stewart, Humphrey Bogart and Bing Crosby. Lastfogel was also Esther Williams' agent. Just after the war, Metro Goldwyn Mayer (MGM) was looking for a new project for Williams—their movie mermaid and highest grossing star. Williams first heard about Annette when she was sent a script called *The One Piece Bathing Suit*. She was used to being given scripts with little or no story and, like Annette, was expected to go through the motions of a performing seal. 'Suddenly I had a script in my hands about a real person. I found tapes of her in *Daughter of the Gods* and I saw why they called her the perfect woman with the perfect body, because she was a swimmer, a real swimmer.'

Williams had never met anyone who she considered a 'real swimmer' before. As she watched the old movie she saw that, though the filming was unsophisticated, Annette was amazingly brave and original. 'If I was unique in 1950, think how unique she was in 1915.' she said.

Annette burst into tears when she learned from Lastfogel that Esther Williams was to play her in a big MGM extravaganza. She'd seen the younger star's remake of *Neptune's Daughter,* which bore no resemblance at all to her film of the same title. There were no fabulous fairy grottos or beautiful mermaids; instead, Esther played a swimsuit manufacturer, and Keenan Wynn was her wisecracking manager.

'I cried so about it,' Annette admitted, 'that at the time I never would have agreed to let them do it. But then I met Esther and I realised she really wanted to do my life story.'

So it was that Abe Lastfogel brought the two most famous women swimmers of their day together. Both had made many millions for the box office and brought water ballet to the big screen. It was Esther Williams, represented by Lastfogel, who initiated the whole idea. She persuaded MGM to buy the rights to 'My Story', to assign Mervyn LeRoy, one of Hollywood's most impressive directors, and to sign up Annette to act as a technical adviser.

In Esther Williams' autobiography, *The Million Dollar Mermaid,* she writes that she met Annette briefly on the set of the movie but never saw her again. When she was later interviewed, Esther elaborated a little more. One day when filming she heard Annette had entered the studio and was on the set. She dismissed the crew and told them not to bother her and Annette for the rest of the day, telling them: 'I want to speak to this wonderful woman.' She remembers Annette standing very straight with her head held high and chin up. She gave Esther an interesting tip: 'You need to stand tall when you have to act without clothes on.'

Despite this helpful hint, Esther sensed Annette's underlying dissatisfaction with her casting and confronted Annette. Annette replied that she wished Williams were Australian. 'I'm the only one in movies who swims and I'll play it as well as I can,' Esther says she told her.

Annette and Esther came from very different backgrounds. Esther was from a poor family and learned to swim in exchange for hiring towels out at the local swimming pool. She learned from a very early age to survive as best she could on her looks. In comparison, Annette's childhood was protected and happy. What brought them together was their love of swimming, which had plucked both of them from their ordinary lives and immersed them in fame and stardom. Annette represented a pinnacle in live entertainment which was soon to be eclipsed by the advent of film, just as Esther's movies were of a type that would in time be eclipsed by television. For both women, swimming was their meditation—a daily ritual to keep anxiety at bay. 'Water is so magic to me and I think it was to Annette too,' says Esther in *The Million Dollar Mermaid*. As Annette did until the end of her life, Esther, now in her late seventies, is still swimming every day. 'It's the only exercise you can do from the first bath to your last without hurting yourself,' she said in her autobiography.

Esther was struck by Annette's bravery and independence— revolutionising swimwear and the English Channel crossing. 'She was way ahead of her time,' she said. But, despite all they had in common, it can't have been a totally comfortable meeting. Esther remembered that Annette was very quiet and then suddenly pulled up her skirts and said: 'Look at these legs!' It was a challenge from one great star to another. 'Swimming muscles,' the other star observed, diffusing the tension. 'I'd know them anywhere.'

It dawned on Williams that no one would be right for the part. Annette's disappointment was that she could not play her younger self. At 65 Annette harboured the idea that she could still take on the role. She actually told reporters she was 'willing to concede that Esther had it from the neck up but from the neck down I concede nothing'. It seems a preposterous idea, but perhaps not if you happen to be a Hollywood star. 'I would probably have had that feeling too,' admitted Williams. 'But there comes a time when the boat sails.'

Annette just couldn't accept the fact of growing old, and did everything she could to keep age at bay. Publicity shots at the time show her touching the ground as she balances on one red stiletto while the other leg is sticking straight up in the air. There's no doubt that she was exceedingly healthy and agile. An admirer from the early days, Vincent X. Flaherty, writing around the time of *Million Dollar Mermaid* was released, says: 'At 65 Annette Kellerman is remarkable. She races up stairs two at a time.'

Though they admired each other when they first met, neither Esther nor Annette was very flattering about the other in later years. In her autobiography, Esther writes of her first meeting with Annette: 'Although she was 65 there was not a wrinkle on her face. She was wearing a scarf with a hat and visor. What she'd done was pull her face up into her hat.' And Annette confided to interviewer Joel Greenberg:

> The beautiful Esther was playing me and I liked her very much. But, you know between you and me, she couldn't dive higher than that bed. When they were making that story I knew everyone, and this girl, who had been Esther's double for ten years, got a thousand dollars per picture. She was very modest. She was an Olympic diver.

And, while Esther found co-star Victor Mature, who played Jimmie, so irresistible that she fell into a torrid love affair with him for the duration of the shoot—'Vic was a strong and fulfilling lover. Better than I had ever fantasized,' she wrote in her autobiography—Annette couldn't stand the man: 'Jimmie is a quiet unassuming husband and I think it is ridiculous that he is being played by that hunk of a man, Victor Mature,' she said. Apparently, when the film came out, poor Jimmie was taunted relentlessly by friends who greeted him with: 'Here comes Samson.' Annette told an interviewer it was 'a namby pamby attempt' to tell her life story. And later she said of *Million Dollar Mermaid,* 'Oh boy, what a silly little yarn that is.' Bosley Crowther of *The New York Times Film Review* agreed:

> This technicolor shindig which laughingly pretends to be a biography of the famous swimmer, Annette Kellerman, is a luxuriance of razzle dazzle that includes Hippodrome sets, water ballets, bathing suit shows, diving performances, low comedy, anachronisms and clichés. It also includes an abundance of Miss Williams and Victor Mature but it does not include the felicities of a reasonably fascinating script . . . the script-writer, Everett Freeman; the director Mervyn LeRoy and occasionally even the actors seem to have strolled out for a smoke. It is in these yawning stretches that *Million Dollar Mermaid* tries to weave the stilted romance that is presented as Miss Kellerman's biography.

Even Esther, who was proud of the movie, admitted that the director, Mervyn LeRoy, was a little 'tired' during filming. He had just finished *Quo Vadis,* a huge and troublesome epic shot in Rome, and wasn't the perceptive director she had expected him to be. According to Esther's autobiography, 'Let's have a nice little scene' was his only direction to his actors, who were otherwise left to muddle through on their own. But Esther was justifiably proud of the aquatic scenes. Even Annette, though she would never have admitted it, must have secretly enjoyed choreographer Busby Berkeley's vision of her *Big Show* at the Hippodrome. Berkeley used more than 100 swimmers, 55-foot high streams of yellow and red smoke, and ramps upon which the swimmers slid into the water while carrying lit torches. Then Williams (or her double) dived from a 50-foot high swing into the mass of swimmers, who immediately went into one of Berkeley's ferris wheel effects (shot from an overhead camera). In the finale, several hundred lit sparklers emerged from the water and formed a backdrop to the ensemble. It was a gaudy but apt tribute to the woman who started it all, and who always loved a chance to make a big spectacular herself.

Though she may not have enjoyed the film, Annette certainly enjoyed time she spent in Hollywood. With her story up on the silver screen she felt like a somebody once more. People had short memories in Tinseltown.

When Annette opened up another health food shop in Long Beach in the early 1950s, not many people recalled the owner as the Perfect Woman of 1907. Opening health food stores seemed to be something of a vogue amongst former action stars. In the late 1940s, Johnny Weissmuller, who had starred as Tarzan only ten years before, also opened a health food store on Sunset Boulevard: 'I don't think most people knew who he was. These people came down in a big way. If you lived long enough, you came back into fashion . . . but most people didn't live long enough,' silent film historian Anthony Slide said in an interview with the author.

Fortunately, Annette did. Suddenly she received invitations from Hollywood celebrities who, because of *Million Dollar Mermaid,* wanted to meet her. She became well acquainted with Walter Pidgeon, who played her father in the film—the only actor she thought was well cast. The role of Alice Charbonnet had been entirely cut from the story. She met Lucille Ball, whom she later described as one of her 'best surviving friends', and Grace Kelly just before her marriage to Prince Rainier. Annette was thrilled to be one of only eighteen women asked to her pre-wedding shower in Hollywood. 'I gave Grace a lace handkerchief given to me by Enrico Caruso. I told her it belonged in a palace. She agreed and wore it at her wedding,' Anette told the *Gold Coast Bulletin*. Annette was interviewed on radio and, for the first time, on television. But the highlight of her stay in Hollywood was an invitation to Pickfair, the prototype for all Hollywood mansions and home of the famous silent stars Mary Pickford and Douglas Fairbanks. Annette was accompanied by Buster Keaton to The Stars' Reunion Party. 'He was a gentleman,' she said later, 'the nicest gentleman I ever met.' Other stars who had survived to enjoy the occasion were popular Latin matinee idol Antonio Moreno, Zazu Pitts, the star of Erich Von Stroheim's *Greed,* and Mae Marsh, one of D.W. Griffiths' favourite lead actresses. There were reporters everywhere, and Annette talked to them all. 'I'm still entertaining,' she told them. 'I sing, I play the accordion and I still do physical culture exercises— look!' At this she bent right over and picked up a carnation from the floor without bending her knees.

But the hype and hoopla of Hollywood and *Million Dollar Mermaid* soon petered out and Annette, not able to face the prospect of going back to her health food business, decided to return to Australia again for the Melbourne Olympics in 1956.

Feted as Australia's first woman swimmer, she was introduced to the crowds in the stadium by Prime Minister Menzies and was cheered loudly. It was here that she met Australia's greatest woman swimmer of the day, Dawn Fraser. When Annette moved to the Gold Coast a few years later, she would swim with Dawn as she trained in the pool at the Chevron Hotel.

Before they left for Australia, Annette and Jimmie visited his sister Cecilia and her family in Minneapolis for one last time. Over the years, they had seen them often. Jimmie's niece, Virginia Gahlbeck, remembers how much they loved it when Annette and Jimmie came to stay. When Virginia and her sister Grace were little girls in Atlanta, Georgia, Annette taught them toe dancing, ballet steps and swimming. Jimmie taught them 'to have spirit and fun in all they did'. After *Million Dollar Mermaid*, Annette and Jimmie came to stay for a month. Virginia described them:

> I have never seen two people so devoted to each other and so interested in everything in life. Every morning, early (they were full of spirit and zest) Annette would practice on the piano or the piano accordion, which she loved. They had a health food breakfast first, then Jimmie would read the paper while she did her really strenuous exercises for some time. Then Jim would prop her arms and legs with pillows while she took her afternoon nap. Then the two would take a long walk. We loved them dearly.

Virginia particularly remembers reading the names of endless exotic places on the stickers plastered all over Jimmie and Annette's travelling trunk, 'there wasn't an inch of space left on it'.

One incident, when the Sullivans were staying at Jimmie's brother Jerry's place, illustrates Annette's own peculiar brand of determination. It took place in 1937, when the age-conscious Annette would have been 51. Jerry, 'who loved to twit people', started a discussion with something he knew would get a reaction—'as you get older you lose your powers of concentration'. Annette jumped up, grabbed a magazine, went to the piano and began playing—'she played beautifully', Virginia recalls— and then started reading the magazine while continuing her conversation with Jerry. She did this for some time and when she had finished Annette told Jerry exactly what she had read and had played and what their conversation was about. He never taunted her again.

Over the years, Jimmie and Annette had regularly dropped in on his family, though now it looked like they would be leaving them for good. As he wrote to his sister Cecilia in 1971, he made this sacrifice for the sake of Annette, 'so she can be close to her sister and relations, as she was away from her homeland for years. I do wish we could be together but fate has decreed Australia'.

17

MOVIE STAR, RETIRED TO THE TROPICS, WISHES TO SELL MINK COAT

Queensland's sub-tropical Gold Coast, like Florida, is the perfect place to retire to. It also has a suburb called Miami and the sun shines all year round. Today, with its miles of glistening beach lined with high rise apartments and steady stream of holiday-makers, it strongly resembles its American cousin. But in the early 1960s when Annette and Jimmie went to live there, the Gold Coast was a quiet retirement area for low-income earners on a modest pension. The houses were typically made of fibro and floors were covered in linoleum—cheap, easy to clean and cool in summer.

The Sullivans decided to settle in a quiet suburb called Labrador. Jimmie was beginning to 'feel the weight of his years'. After keeping up for so long with what Mipps called 'that female dynamo', he was ready to take life a little more slowly. But, though she applied the brakes a little to keep him company, Annette was not ready to come to a full stop. Once they settled in, she found out where the action was for her age group (she was now in her early seventies) and joined the newly formed

Geranium Club. She was already very fond of geraniums, as she had grown them in her garden in Los Angeles, but quickly became an expert, attending meetings every week and corresponding with the very well-established London Geranium Club which eventually named a beautiful dark-red geranium after her. Annette discovered who the movers and shakers were in Labrador and shook them up a little more, proposing numerous shows and parades to raise money for local clubs, nursing homes and charities. She organised historical bathing suit pageants, with the swimwear modelled by reluctant young recruits. She hosted lunches and dinners and, if she couldn't find a worthy cause, would go ahead with a raffle anyway. Paula Stafford, a well-known swimsuit designer who introduced the Gold Coast to the bikini, remembers being asked to a dinner party at Annette's house:

> She had one lovely trick, she'd have a party for about eight people and she'd say 'I'm going to have a raffle!' And we'd say 'how much?' and she'd say, 'Oh there's no charge for the tickets.' But she'd always make sure I won. And I've still got a cushion cover that I won from one of her marvellous no pay raffles for no charity and no money. She was priceless!

When she first came to the Gold Coast, Annette would swim every day in the pool at the Chevron Hotel, the smartest hotel in town. Jimmie's footage of Annette in her seventies shows her in a red swimsuit that covers her arms and legs. She slowly glides through the water, practising her perfect Australian crawl and pausing to wave to camera. After her laps, she finishes off with her physical culture routine. Paula Stafford remembers people at the pool asking who she was. 'You'd say, "Annette Kellerman".

And they'd say, "Who's Annette Kellerman?" Most people in the area knew her only as "the little old lady of Labrador".'

Stafford thought it a shame that Annette wasn't recognised in Australia. She was impressed by the older woman: 'She was always entertaining and had great energy and with it all a certain modesty.' Annette liked to talk about the highlights of her career but, according to Stafford, 'she wasn't boasting, she was telling, which is very different. She had an innate modesty. She was quite a remarkable person, I thought.'

Annette could never get used to the idea that no one knew, or even wanted to know, who she was. She told the *Gold Coast Weekly* in 1974:

> I think it is terrible the way Australian stars make a big name for themselves overseas yet come back here and are virtually looked down on. Australians ignore talented performers who were bred here and prefer to watch the likes of Frank Sinatra.

In 1970, when Jimmie caught the Asian flu, Annette was too absorbed in looking after him to worry about her reputation. She was content to spend more and more time with her husband, but he never really recovered. A year later he was trying to reassure his sister in a letter: 'It has weakened me but still I'm normally healthy at my age, you know I'm 86. Still look sick but feel well.'

Adding a line or two at the end of his letter, Annette is still very positive: 'The doctor says his *lungs* and heart are *very* good.' Her bold sprawling hand, full of flourish and flair, exclamation marks and underlinings, is a contrast to Jimmie's small, neat, thoughtful scratchings. It reveals more about their relationship than any photograph could.

Jimmie hung on for a year or more, probably because of his wife's willpower more than his own. 'Annette is always wonderful and keeps me going when I am ready to give up . . . I love her so much,' he wrote in his last letter to his sister.

During these last months, Jimmie took things very quietly, but finally, in the middle of the cyclone season, Annette wrote to her sister-in-law:

> My darling Jimmie has passed away—he died in his sleep! Thank God! People loved him. As for me! Sixty years together. He was a wonderful husband and help mate. Jim had a very happy life with me. We lived for one another! We were never separated. At present I am a lost soul.

Annette was really unable to function after Jimmy died, she was truly lost. Jimmie's niece Virginia remembers them 'just as much in love at the end of their lives as at the beginning'. Mipps persuaded her sister to move into her home in Angler's Paradise. There, almost at the end of her life, Annette had to start all over again. For the first time in her life, she was on her own. According to Mipps, Annette managed because, for her, 'crises were made to be surmounted'. She was 86 and, though she had stopped swimming while Jimmie was sick, she again began to take an active role in charity work and continued her exercise regime every morning: 'She would as soon miss her breakfast as her strenuous workout,' Mipps said in 'Let's Do Something'.

Though her sister was there to look after her, Annette was never the same after Jimmie's death. 'When he died it was awful,' she told Joel Greenberg, almost angrily. 'Sixty years is too long really to be married to one person but we got on so well.' Kitch Robinson, a friend who visited Annette at Mipps' house, recalls a small fibro house with linoleum floors and not much furniture. It was there she first saw Annette's mink coat. There are two versions to this next part of the story. According to Annette, Kitch offered to sell the coat for her and Annette agreed, telling her 'if you do I'll give you half'. However, Kitch Robinson says Annette asked her to sell it because she needed the cash.

The incident brings up the whole question of what happened to the money that Annette made throughout her career, a career where she excelled in places like the Hippodrome in New York and the Coliseum in London, and where she was paid one of the highest wages in vaudeville. As one of the biggest earning film stars of her day, she also continued with her lucrative sideline on the lecture circuit, educating women about the benefits of physical culture and swimming. One journalist early in Annette's career estimated that she was well on the way to becoming one of the richest women in showbusiness. Both Annette and Jimmie, at different times in their later years, insisted that they were well off. 'After all, to get to the age of 88, you've got to have plenty of money, it's got to last,' Annette told Joel Greenberg. 'Everything I did was touched with good money.' In the last few months of his life, Jimmie assured his sister: 'Please note, Cecilia dear, that we are both physically and financially independent—our finances are so arranged that we have the independence that comes with proper financial holdings—that we took care of a long time ago.'

However, people who met Annette when she was living with her sister remember them as not too well off. Jo Stolkowski knew Mipps and Annette well in Anglers Paradise and remembers them living very meagrely. He would drive the sisters around and often bring them gifts of fruit and vegetables. If there had been any money, Annette would certainly have shared it with her sister, who was only surviving on a war widow's pension.

Maybe Annette and Jimmie didn't want to worry their relatives, or perhaps they were just proud. It could be that they lost money during the Depression, as by that time Annette had accumulated her fortune, but it seems unlikely, as the Sullivans travelled the world first class throughout that period and afterwards. The more probable explanation for a lack of funds was the war work Jimmie and Annette did. Annette proudly admitted in 'My Story' that, with their own money, they funded all the tours of the RCTU up and down the east coast of Australia for most of the war. Though she stated in the program for *We're All In It* that 'Miss Kellerman donates all costumes, scenery, musical score, libretto and her own services at no cost whatsoever to the Red Cross', not all the cast of 60 were volunteers. The Kellermanettes performed for free, but the musicians and dancers were professional and on top of their usual wage would have been eligible for a touring fee. Five years of putting on free shows with a cast of 60 must have made a dent in their savings. There is also a mysterious letter of thanks from the American Centre 'for donations' made to them in 1945. There is no mention of the sum involved but the Sullivans were notoriously generous to those less fortunate than themselves.

In the winter of 1974 Kitch Robinson put an advertisement in the *Sydney Morning Herald* classifieds: 'Movie Star, retired to the Gold Coast, no longer has need for mink coat.' There was an overwhelming response with everyone wanting to know whose mink coat it was. Eventually she sold the coat for $600 to a woman who wore it to the opening of the new Sydney Opera House, which is where, coincidentally, Annette bequeathed her theatrical wardrobe. The advertisement also intrigued journalists, who made inquiries. Stories began to appear about Annette. At 89 she was discovered once again, and suddenly became a cherished national treasure.

A television drama for ABC TV's *Behind the Legends* series was written about Annette. The publicity also led to an advertisement being placed in the *Sydney Morning Herald* asking for anyone who could supply the address of Miss Annette Kellerman. An unknown acquaintance obliged and a week later a letter arrived from Buck Dawson, who had been searching for Annette for months: 'At LAST we have found your address. We are pleased to inform you that you are being inducted into the International Swimming Hall of Fame.' Presidential nominee Barry Goldwater and famous talk show host Art Linkletter were to be the guest speakers at this Oscars night of swimming. Also being honoured were two other Australians—Mina Wylie, an Australian national champion for twenty consecutive years, and Alick Wickham, first exponent of the Australian crawl and pioneering surfer.

'Please Annette,' wrote Dawson, 'don't think you are too old to come! We *must* have you here!' She telegraphed back: 'Coming *stop* Happy to be with you again *stop* Annette.' She made plans to visit the United States for one last time. 'The sweetest part,' wrote Mipps in 'Let's Do Something', 'was that she had really been remembered.' Congratulations came from all over Australia. Annette was as excited as a schoolgirl at the thought of seeing her old friends and being the star attraction at the induction ceremony. Not only was she was looking forward to being met at the airport by Esther Williams, but she was also thrilled that Jimmie's beautiful film of her Silver Springs underwater adagio was to open the ceremony. Unfortunately, a month before she was due to leave she stumbled and fell hard on the concrete patio, injuring her leg. The disappointment and 'complete shock to her already over-excited nervous system' (Mipps' words) made her unable to travel. While she was laid up with her leg, Mipps was discreetly approached by *This is Your Life*. Hoping she would be well enough, preparations went ahead for the show in May 1975, but Annette's health didn't improve. She couldn't understand why, after all her physical exercises, she couldn't get well. Just weeks before her fall, she had had energy to spare when she organised *The Creative Nostalgia Parade of the Scintillating Past* on the Gold Coast. Though she was nearly 90 Annette felt indestructible and, despite her injuries, still believed she could regain her strength—if she could just put on 1 kilogram she could restore her perfect body. So she dragged herself from her bed and tried to do her physical culture routine.

'She would go out into the garden again and again and fall each time, just to prove to herself and us that she could walk and get around,' recalled Mipps. 'We could not argue with her . . . we would just pick her up again.'

In the end, the body of the Perfect Woman so betrayed her that the doctor had to send Annette to hospital. Mipps had her placed in the public ward, ostensibly because Annette didn't want to be alone, but perhaps also because they just couldn't afford anything else. Her indomitable restlessness never left her and the nurses found her constantly trying to crawl out of bed. Even at this stage of her life Annette still made an impression. Marjorie Fawcett, one of her nurses remembers, 'caring for Annette was a joy', and that 'her tiny feet still had the arch of a ballerina'. When she was transferred to a nursing home suffering from pneumonia, to the surprise of the nurses and her doctor she enjoyed the fuss everyone made of her and held on a little longer. Her strong lungs and steady heart kept beating until, on the 6 November 1975, she quietly closed her eyes for the last time.

Gold Coast life savers were Annette's pallbearers. From the air, her ashes were set free over her beloved Barrier Reef. Amongst floral tributes, they wafted down over Kennedy Sound, into the Coral Sea below.

For almost 90 years, Annette had never resisted a challenge. When she wanted to do something, she went ahead and did it— tightrope walking, driving cars, playing tennis, horse riding, fencing, acting, ballet, playing the piano and the piano accordion, singing and songwriting—she mastered them all. For Annette, nothing succeeded like success.

Water remained the element that ran through Annette's life from the time she shed her callipers to take her first tentative swimming lesson to her last lap of the Chevron Hotel pool. She made her name in the waters of the English Channel and made her fortune in her 25 000 gallon tank. She and her mermaids charmed the world as they flicked their tails on the silver screen and dived into the deep blue sea. Water made her a star; it was both her inspiration and her sanity.

> Water always teaches me a new story . . . and swimming is a benefit—a clean cool beautiful thing we all, from cats to kings, can enjoy. The man who has not given himself completely to the sun and wind and cold sting of the waves will never know all the meanings of life. The love of the unknown is the greatest of all the joys which swimming has for me . . . I am still looking for my chest of gold in a cool, dripping sea cave . . . I still wait to see my first real mermaid sitting on a damp grey rock combing her long green hair.

ACKNOWLEDGEMENTS

Emily Gibson

I'd like to thank Barbara Firth for giving me access to her collection and her unique personal knowledge, without which I could never have written this book. Many thanks also to Peter Byers and Anne Gibson for their counselling skills, Rob Gibson for legal advice, Ian Collie and Hilton Cordell for access to their information and images, Shirley Jaffe for her hospitality in New York and LA, Alex McGregor for steering me in the right direction when I was driving on the wrong side of the road, Anne Zahalka for her photos and Jorge Pereira for keeping me going with his consistently delicious culinary delights.

Barbara Firth

Since 1975 the following people and organisations have contributed their knowledge, practical help and interest in my research endeavours, and I am sincerely grateful to them: Academy of Motion Picture Arts and Sciences (Margaret Herrick Library),

Maisie Anderson, Jill Antill-Rose, Arts Law Centre of Australia, Australian National Maritime Museum (Members), Meg Bartlett, Edward Bell, *Boston Herald* (John Cronin), Boston and Weston Public Libraries, Joanna Boulken, Brisbane Water (NSW) Legacy, Avril Brockett, Canterbury Public Library, Peter Collas, Ian Collie, David Cowell, Harry Cox—(librarian, *Daily Mirror*, London), Jenny Dixon-Elliott, Dr Elizabeth Elliott, John and Beverley Elliott, Emerson College (Bob Fleming), Marjorie Fawcett, Samuel E. Fry (US State Dept), Virginia Gahlbeck, Emily Gibson, Captain David Guthrie, Natalie Guy, Blanche Hanalis, Raymond Hartley, Dr Joan Hult (Maryland University), International Swimming Hall of Fame (Don de Bolt, Marion Washburn), Annette Kellerman, Library of Congress, Peter McCauley, Mitzi Mogul, Museum of Modern Art (Charles Silver), National Council of Women of USA (Merinelle Sullivan, Dr Ruth Schellberg, Claire Friedland), National Councils of Women of Australia and New South Wales, New York Public Library (Don Madison, Dorothy Swerdlove), Michael Overland (Queensland Parks & Wildlife), Prudence Robinson, Valerie Robinson, Schlesinger Library—Harvard University, Screensound Australia (Simon Drake), State Library of New South Wales (Paul Brunton), Sydney Opera House (Frank Barnes, Lloyd Ravenscroft, Paul Bentley), Marilyn Young, Anne and Don Reynolds, University of Southern California—Doheny Library (Ned Comstock), Jozef Szalkowski, War Widows' Guild of Australia (NSW), Phyllis White, Esther Williams, Marcelle Wooster, Mildred Yates.

This biography is dedicated to the memory of two remarkable sisters, Annette Kellerman and Marcelle Wooster. Without the wonderful support and interest of my late husband, Gordon, and our daughters, Debbie and Cathy, my 29 years of intermittent Australian and overseas research would not have been possible.

SOURCES

CHAPTER 1

I want you to carry this figure (p. 4) *Boston Commercial*, 28 December 1909.

I'm perfectly healthy that's all (p. 4) *Washington Times*, 3 October 1909.

I think it was this tenacity (p. 14) Marcelle Wooster interviewed by Peter Luck, 1976.

I prefer long distances (p. 17) *the Australasian*, 30 April 1904.

CHAPTER 3

I don't want you making a fool (p. 36) *The American Magazine*, March 1917.

Wolffe tried a series of different strategies (p. 37) Jarvis (1975).

Lady and gentleman stood up (p. 38) *Daily Mirror*, 31 July 1905.

Annette was still using the double-armed (p. 38) International Swimming Hall of Fame website at ♣www.ishof.org♣.

She started with a powerful double-armed stroke (p. 38) *Daily Mirror*, 31 July 1905.

No fewer than five plucky (p. 39) *Daily Mirror*, 25 August 1905.

I'll propose to you (p. 40) *Daily Mirror*, 25 August 1905.

Diving had only recently (p. 42) Sprawlson (2000).

By the time Annette arrived in London (p. 43) Sims (1902).

She performed in what was described as (p. 44) Sims (1902).

There is that in Miss Kellerman's display (p. 45) *The London Spectator*, 2 April 1906.

I shall be unhappy till I meet her (p. 46) Nelson (1991)

CHAPTER 5

Being the perfect woman antagonises (p. 61) Newspaper article (name and date unknown).

225

Mrs Pattee's complaint averred (p. 62) *Philadelphia Herald*, 1909.

CHAPTER 6

There's a new Venus in town (p. 66) *New York Star*, 26 December 1908.

We believed in soap and water (p. 67) DiMeglio (1973).

In Keith's theatres there were signs (p. 67) Ergman (2004).

It is something quite apart (p. 68) *Pittsburgh Telegraph*, 21 September 1909.

The mayor of East Liverpool NY (p. 68) *Pittsburgh Telegraph*, 24 January 1915.

The insurance company reportedly said (p. 69) *New York Telegraph*, 6 March 1910.

For instance, when someone in government (p. 69) *New York Telegraph*, 7 March 1910.

Miss Kellerman has won a unique distinction (p. 71) *Variety* (date unknown).

Acts were booked centrally (p. 71) Ergman (2004).

One newspaper reported her (p. 72) *New York Star*, 17 April 1909.

On the bill that night in Pittsburgh (p. 73) *Pittsburgh Despatch*, 21 September 1909.

Miss Kellerman wants a chauffeur (p. 74) *New York Telegraph*, 29 June 1909.

A big touring car approached (p. 75) *New York Telegraph*, 30 July 1909.

There is no pleasure in life greater (p. 76) Newspaper (name unknown) 1 May 1910.

Chere petite (p. 78) *Pittsburgh Leader* (p. 78) 9 September 1909.

When she was about to make a second dive (p. 78) *Indianapolis Star*, 3 January 1909.

I like to please people (p. 78) *Indianapolis Star*, 3 January 1909.

Naturally the young lady posed (p. 82) *New York Herald*, 15 August 1909.

According to the New York Telegraph (p. 84) *New York Telegraph*, 11 May 1909.

Her fans were just as keen (p. 84) *New York Telegraph*, 12 May 1909.

The Queen of Modern Vaudeville (p. 84) Slide (1994).

Not long after (p. 85) *New York Sun*, 28 June 1909.

A rush of fat folk to the sea (p. 86) *New York Telegraph* (date unknown).

CHAPTER 7

She does not wear the thing (p. 90) *Pittsburgh Leader*, 24 September 1909.

When I say exercise and diet (p. 91) *Pittsburgh Leader* (date unknown).

I always advocate something to do (p. 92) *New York Evening Journal*, 1 May 1912.

The average woman takes it as a matter of course (p. 94) *Syracuse Post Standard* (date unknown).

Long before yoga had become popular (p. 95) *New York Evening Journal*, 1 May 1912.

Some of Miss Kellerman's clothes (p. 96) *New York Telegraph*, 29 May 1910.

She will wear a lampshade (p. 97) *Atlanta Georgian*, 25 March 1911.

CHAPTER 8

The perfect woman approaches the ocean (p. 102) *New York Telegraph* (date unknown).

CHAPTER 9

Either Annette Kellerman is the greatest (p. 115) Slide (1994)

Unable to find an actor who could also (p. 119) Interview with Joel Greenberg.

As both fell, Mr Brenon's head (p. 119) *Baltimore News*, 18 January 1914.

Three months later, the film opened (p. 122) *New York Review*, 18 April 1914.

The finest picture ever shown (p. 122) *New York Telegraph*, 28 April 1914.

The biggest film feature (p. 122) *Atlanta Georgian*, 23 June 1914.

Squads of police were present (p. 123) *Chicago Tribune*, 19 May 1914.

Never before in the annals of picturedom (p. 123) *Pittsburgh Leader*, 26 July 1914.

It was demonstrated to the lovers (p. 124) *Buffalo Times*, 23 August 1914.

I'm tired of flopping into tanks (p. 124) *Detroit News*, 10 May 1914.

CHAPTER 10

At that time Hollywood (p. 129) Interview with Joel Greenberg.

The inhabitants of Jamaica fear rabies (p. 132) *New York Star*, 25 November 1916.

In the case of Daughter of the Gods (p. 134) *Evening Wisconsin*, 4 February 1917.

A miniature village sprang up (p. 134) *Detroit News*, 18 January 1917.

We engaged the children from babes-in-arms (p. 134) *Detroit News*, 17 December 1917.

The fabric didn't last long (p. 135) *Detroit News*, 13 January 1917.

Riding her black horse Pluto (p. 135) *Motion Picture Classic*, February 1917.

According to the Toledo Blade (p. 136) *Toledo Blade*, 12 January 1917.

They were about to abandon (p. 137) *Motion Picture Classic*, February 1917.

I rode ahead of them (p. 137) Interview with Joel Greenberg.

Yet from Annette down (p. 138) Thompson (1996)

We'd go out on these long treks (p. 139) Interview with Joel Greenberg.

They were going to throw a dummy in (p. 140) Interview with Joel Greenberg.

He went up to Herbert and said (p. 141) Interview with Joel Greenberg.

He was just over ambitious (p. 141) Interview with Joel Greenberg.

A real Jewish business man (p. 143) Interview with Joel Greenberg.

She was one of those mothers (p. 143) Interview with Joel Greenberg.

What does 1,000,000 or a million (p. 143) Newspaper article (name and date unknown).

Jimmie was quiet and reliable (p. 144) Interview with Joel Greenberg.

When I go to the theatre (p. 145) *Cincinnati Herald*, 18 May, 1916.

The wise manager will not overlook (p. 146) *New York Dramatic News*, June 1917.

Professor Carl Sloertzer of Leipzig (p. 147) *Atlanta Constitution*, 31 May 1916.

Many scenes in which Miss Kellerman (p. 147) Thompson (1996, p. 59).

Aubrey Munson (p. 148) Thompson (1996, p. 60).

I had a very thin pair of tights (p. 148) Interview with Joel Greenberg.

A pitiful sight when he appeared (p. 148) *Toledo Blade* (date unknown).

Those who contend that woman is too (p. 149) *New York Times Journal*, 19 October 1916.

She displays a courage (p. 149) *Boston Post* (date unknown).

With almost kaleidoscopic swiftness (p. 149) *New York Dramatic News*, 28 October 1916.

Its loss is tragic (p. 150) Thompson (1996, p. 60).

There is a shot that reveals Annette (p. 150) Margaret Herrick collection, Academy of Motion Picture Arts and Sciences Library.

It has a touch of The Birth of a Nation (p. 151) *Motion Picture News*, November 1917.

Exhibited in the history of cinema (p. 151) *Louisville Herald*, January 1917.

A film like Daughter of the Gods (p. 151) Interview with Frank Thompson.

I don't have anything at all (p. 152) Interview with Joel Greenberg.

What is known is that (p. 151) *New York Mail*, 19 December 1916.

Let us return to our mother's knees (p. 152) Thompson (1996).

Here and there I recognized a Wagnerian (p. 152) *Motion Picture News*, November 1917.

As grand a tale of nereids and necromancy (p. 152) Thompson (1996).

Considered as a play or a plot (p. 152) *Boston Transcript*, 19 October 1916.

Both the president and Mrs Wilson (p. 153) *Chicago Herald*, 19 December 1916.

She was lead out in front (p. 153) *Pittsburgh Leader*, 26 October 1916.

CHAPTER 11

I was 60–70 feet up (p. 155) Interview with Joel Greenberg.

She practised and waited days (p. 156) New York Telegraph, 30 September 1917.

Watching the making of Queen of the Seas (p. 160) New York Telegraph (date unknown).

The film will be entirely different in action (p. 161) New York American, 13 August 1917.

With her hair cut in a fashionable (p. 161) Dramatic Mirror, 14 August 1920.

I was playing one of those women (p. 161) Interview with Joel Greenberg.

CHAPTER 12

She would have ended up as a Tarzan (p. 166) Interview with Joel Greenberg.

The little Australian Lady doesn't suffer (p. 167) Rochester Post, 31 January 1910.

I have spent thousands of dollars (p. 167) Newspaper article (name and date unknown).

She also attempts to sing (p. 168) Cincinnati Everyman, 9 May 1915.

She was found to possess art (p. 168) Toledo Blade, 29 March 1915.

A large glass tank set in the centre (p. 171) New York Journal, 29 January 1918.

Surrounded by a gorgeous setting (p. 172) Variety, 20 January 1917.

On all sides of Broadway (p. 172) New York Telegraph, 29 January 1917.

Not that Miss Kellerman expects her admirers (p. 173) New York Telegraph, 4 May 1917.

Everything they are interested in (p. 174) Motion Picture Classic, February 1917.

Though magazines ran photos of Annette (p. 174) Photoplay, April 1917.

The major interest of the act (p. 174) Milwaukee Missouri News, 9 January 1919.

A water witch that her perfect figure (p. 175) Boston Time, 12 March 1918.

The machine was brought within forty (p. 175) Photoplay, September 1919.

She published her book (p. 175) Kansas City Star, 24 September 1919.

Adequate public bathing facilities (p. 176) Fort Wayne News, 9 August 1916.

Miss Kellerman was discovered sitting on the end (p. 176) Picture Play Magazine, August 1918.

CHAPTER 13

The famous mermaid on making her first appearance (p. 185) New York American, 29 January 1927.

CHAPTER 14

Our home and work are in New York (p. 194) Walkabout, 1949.

CHAPTER 15

Who's behind the Union Jack? (p. 197) James Sullivan, 'Annette Kellerman as I Knew Her', unpublished manuscript.

She recalled her still being very supple (p. 199) Letter to Barbara Firth.

Well she still weighs 125 lbs (p. 201) Variety (date unknown).

Mothers and fathers of these servicemen (p. 201) Evening News Baltimore, 6 September 1944.

Miss Kellerman put the crowd into good humour (p. 202) Newspaper article (name and date unknown).

Five hundred elaborate costumes (p. 202) Sunday Guardian Sun, 5 February 1940.

A dear little man (p. 204) Gold Coast News, 1 September 1974.

The most god awful trip (p. 204) Gold Coast Courier, (date unknown).

CHAPTER 16

Suddenly I had a script in my hands (p. 205) Transcript of interview with Esther Williams for documentary The Original

Mermaid (Hilton Cordell Productions, 2002).

I cried so about it (p. 206) *Los Angeles Times*, 23 March 1952.

Willing to concede that Esther had it from the neck up (p. 208) *Los Angeles Times*, 23 March 1952.

A namby pamby attempt (p. 209) *Gold Coast Weekly*, 1974.

Oh boy, what a silly little yarn (p. 209) Interview with Joel Greenberg.

I gave Grace a lace handkerchief (p. 211) *Gold Coast Bulletin*, 17 November 1975.

He was a gentleman (p. 211) Interview with Joel Greenberg.

I have never seen two people so devoted (p. 212) Letter to Barbara Firth.

CHAPTER 17

Caring for Annette was a joy (p. 221) Letter to Barbara Firth.

Water always teaches me a new story (p. 222) Kellerman (1918, p. 36).

BIBLIOGRAPHY

Bodeen, De Witt and Holland, Larry (no date), 'Neptune's Daughters: Annette Kellerman and Esther Williams', *Films in Review*.

DiMeglio, John E. 1973, *Vaudeville, USA*, Bowling Green University Popular Press, Bowling Green, Ohio.

Curtis, Emerson R. 1949, 'There Was a Peace on Newry Island', *Walkabout*, Melbourne.

Ergman, Andrew L. 2004, *Blue Vaudeville: Sex, Morals and the Mass Marketing of Amusement, 1895–1915*, McFarland and Co., Jefferson, NC.

Greenberg, Joel 1975, Interview with Annette Kellerman, unpublished.

Jarvis, Margaret A. 1975, *Captain Webb and 100 Years of Channel Swimming*, David and Charles Newton Abbot, Devon.

Kellerman, Annette, 'My Story', unpublished autobiography, held at State Library of New South Wales, Sydney.

Kellerman, Annette 1926, *Fairy Tales of the South Seas and Other Stories*, illustrated by Marcelle Wooster, Sampson Low Marsten, London.

Kellerman, Annette 1918, *How to Swim*, Heinemann, London.

Kellerman, Annette 1918, *Physical Beauty: How to Keep It*, Doran, New York.

Nelson, Judy 1991, 'The Forgotten Mermaid', *Wonderful Women of OZ*, Sydney.

Sims, George R. 1903, *Living London*, Cassell and Co., London.

Slide, Anthony 1994, *The Encyclopedia of Vaudeville*, Greenwood Press, Wesport.

Sprawlson, Charles 2000, *Haunts of the Black Masseur: The Swimmer as Hero*, University of Minnesota Press, Minneapolis.

Thompson, Frank 1996, *Lost Films: Important Movies That Disappeared*, Carol Publishing, Secausus, NJ.

Williams, Esther 1999, *The Million Dollar Mermaid: An Autobiography*, Simon and Schuster, New York.

Wooster, Marcelle, 'Let's Do Something', unpublished autobiography, held at State Library of New South Wales, Sydney.